FLAT BACK FOUR

FLAT BACK FOUR

The Tactical Game

Andy Gray with Jim Drewett

BOXTREE

First published in Great Britain in hardback 1998 by Boxtree

This edition published 1999 by Boxtree
an imprint of Macmillan Publishers Ltd
25 Eccleston Place London SW1W 9NF
and Basingstoke

Associated companies throughout the world

ISBN 0 7522 1196 X

9 8 7 6 5 4 3 2 1

A CIP catalogue record for this book is available from
the British Library.

Typeset by SX Composing DTP, Rayleigh, Essex

Printed by Mackays of Chatham PLC, Chatham, Kent

Contents

● ●

Key to Illustrations

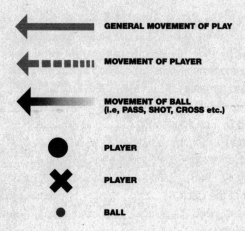

GENERAL MOVEMENT OF PLAY

MOVEMENT OF PLAYER

MOVEMENT OF BALL
(i.e, PASS, SHOT, CROSS etc.)

PLAYER

PLAYER

BALL

Acknowledgements

I'd like to pay tribute to all the managers I ever played under. Everything I learned – good or bad – came from them. So thanks to Jim McLean, Ron Saunders, John Barnwell, Ian Greaves, Graham Hawkins, Howard Kendall, Graham Turner, Billy McNeill, Ron Atkinson, Graeme Souness, Willie Ormond, Ally McLeod, Jock Stein and Alex Ferguson.

Andy Gray

Special thanks to Andy, whose deep knowledge and unbounded enthusiasm for the game of football made my job easy, and to Sarah for all the sandwiches. To Jenny Olivier for her encouragement and flexibility with the deadline and Mary Pachnos for getting the ball rolling in the first place. Thanks also to the other members of Deadline Features' very own flat back four: 'keepy uppy' champion Clive Batty for his meticulous research, Matthew Hirtes, and my business partner Alex Leith for keeping the company above water and reminding me there are two 'b's in Grobbelaar. A special mention also to Jonathan Sim and Rachel Jeffries at Sky Sports for their help which, as always, went beyond the call of duty; to Duke Mettle for producing the diagrams; to the players of Cottenham Park FC for their constant willingness to experiment with tactics, usually unintentionally, in the Leatherhead and District League Division Six; and to Suzy for putting up with the growling ogre who lived in the office under the stairs for six weeks.

Jim Drewett

FOREWORD
by Ron Atkinson

● ●

Andy Gray has become one of the most respected men in football when it comes to talking tactics and systems. He has a deep knowledge of the game and an uncanny way of being able to explain things clearly. It's obvious that he's learnt from the right people...well, he was my assistant manager at Aston Villa before going full time with Sky Sports.

Like Andy, I suppose I would describe myself as a student of the game. Having been involved in football nearly all my life – as a player with Aston Villa and Oxford United and a manager in England and Spain – it has been fascinating to see how tactics and systems have evolved from the days of Stanley Matthews, baggy shorts and the 'WM' formation to the modern game where there are more variations of 4–4–2 than there are Italian internationals on the Chelsea subs' bench.

I remember that when I was a manager in Spain the reporters were only interested in the formation we were going to play – would we play a back line of four or a pressing midfield? Over here the newspapers are still much more interested in who's had a bust-up with who on the training ground or how much so-and-so is earning. So, when it comes to appreciating exactly what's happening on the pitch during a tight, tactical game of football most fans in this country still have a long way to go. But with Andy Gray going strong that can't last for long.

Nowadays anyone and everyone wants to talk about flat back fours, sweeper systems and what have you, but many of them don't really know what they are going on about. This book should go some way to changing that. It explains everything, but in a way that doesn't make you feel like you've just sat through a three-hour physics lecture.

So settle down with this book between matches or even during the half-time break, and you'll soon be amazed how much a deeper knowledge of the game heightens your enjoyment of football. I might even have to start referring to it next time Sheffield Wednesday are 1–0 down at Hillsborough.

INTRODUCTION

• •

From as early as I can remember I have been football mad. At the age of eight and already a regular on the terraces at Ibrox, I was captivated by everything around me. The surge of the crowd and the mighty roar as Rangers emerged from the tunnel put me in dreamland. It wasn't a complicated game I watched from those heaving, baying terraces. Rangers kicked off every match and tried to score more goals than the other team. They usually succeeded and that was that. I knew they had two wingers, a big number nine, a back four and a goalkeeper but that was about it. It was all I needed to know. I doubt I had ever even heard the word 'tactics'. I certainly didn't know what it meant. But I stood there open-mouthed, spellbound by the twenty-two men chasing a ball around on that glorious green pitch. It was just about as good as it could ever get.

Or so I thought. For how ever much I daydreamed, how could I have known that one day I myself would be privileged enough to be one of those twenty-two men running themselves into the ground in front of 50,000 on the Ibrox turf? Little did I realise that football would slowly reveal itself to me to be not just the simplest, purest game on earth, but something that was at the same time as strategic and complex as chess or poker.

And now – after more than 500 professional matches, 224 goals for six clubs and twenty caps for my country – I am considered, by my employers at Sky Television at least, to be an authority on the game. I don't pretend to have a deeper knowledge of football than the next man, much of what I say is opinion and speculation, but I do have the experience of playing the game at the highest level. I've been lucky enough to win league titles, FA, League and European Cup Winners' Cup medals under some of the game's great managers, and it's the knowledge and the experience that I picked up along that incredible footballing journey that has led me to this discussion of tactics and systems.

Football is one of the simplest games on earth, yet it's one which most of us have studied more than we ever did our maths and geography books at school. The fact that all you need for a game is a ball, a pitch, twenty-two players and two goals, effectively turns the football pitch before every game into a blank canvas. Like a game of chess, at the start all things are even. All things are uniform. But no two chess games are ever the same. No two chess players have ever made the same moves for an entire game. When Kasparov and Karpov sit down to play, it is not just two blokes passing the time of day, it's a battle of minds, a battle of nerves and wits. In the same way, when Italy line up against Brazil in a World Cup Final, it's a meeting of styles, of cultures and histories. It's a meeting of the minds of their coaches and the wits of the players. That is why for millions of people around the world football is more than a mere game, it's an obsession and a way of life. Throw in the drama, spectacle and beauty and football is truly a subject worth studying...well, it is at least worth a night's discussion in the pub, with glasses for goals and beer mats for players.

Whether it's a team packed full of world-class international players or one that hoofs the ball around the park on a Sunday morning, every team has a system. Every game has a tactical element. That's what this book is about. I don't expect managers and coaches to rush out and buy a copy thinking it will teach them everything they need to know. It's more a guide for the supporter who stands on the terraces or sits in the stands. These days I think your average fan turns up at the game and, after hearing the team line-ups announced, says, 'Right, how are we playing today? Are we playing 4–3–3? Oh, no we're not, we're playing 4–4–2 but Teddy Sheringham is just dropping off to play "in the hole".'

Football as a game has evolved just as the tastes and requirements of its audience have, and it has been tremendous for me to look back on some of the great games and analyse the great teams of the past. I've looked at how Hungary's tactics in beating England 6–3 in 1953 to become the first foreign side to defeat them at Wembley changed the game of football. I've studied England's 'wingless wonders' of 1966, Brazil's samba style of the 1970 World Cup and AC Milan's pressing game of the 1980s. It is fascinating to see how, by introducing anything from offside traps to sweeper systems, pressing midfields and lone strikers, football managers and coaches have taken their teams – and the game – forward.

This isn't supposed to be some sort of textbook or unreadable training manual. By reflecting on some of my own memories and experiences from my playing career and by drawing on some of what I have learned by analysing the Premiership so closely for Sky Sports in recent years, I intend to provide a light and lively insight into the tactics of the modern game and to see what we can learn from the great teams of the past. I'll even put my neck on the line and reveal the system I believe to be the best in football, the system I would have my team playing if I was ever to hang up my squiggly Sky pen and take up football management.

I hope that this book increases your understanding and appreciation of the modern game and goes some way towards explaining how the football that you see on Sky Sports has evolved. Most of all, however, I hope you enjoy it.

CHAPTER 1
The Beginning: Early Tactics and Systems

● ●

One of the earliest recorded games of organised football in Britain took place on Shrove Tuesday in Chester in the tenth century. About as far away from a modern clash between, say, Manchester United and Liverpool as you could possibly get, the match featured around 500 'players', two goals literally miles apart and, if the legend is to be believed, the head of a Danish viking as a ball. There were no offside traps, no wing backs and no setpieces – well, there were no rules – and the match became so violent that it had to be abandoned with the score still at 0–0. A more sedate running race was held instead. The world's greatest game, however, had been born.

The roots of football go back even further than that famously fearsome tussle on the cobbled streets of Chester. There might not have been much in the way of tactics involved, but it seems that almost as soon as humans made the evolutionary jump from pure hunters into farmers and craftsmen we began doing what comes naturally when a light, spherical object is placed at our feet – kicking it.

As early as 200 BC a form of football known as *tsu-chu* ('kicking the ball with the feet') was played with a leather ball in China. Indeed, the first ever international match – always thought to be the England v Scotland encounter in 1872 – may well have been played more than 2,000 years earlier, by China and Japan. The Munich Ethnological Museum in West Germany contains a text by Li-Ju, a Chinese writer who lived around 50 BC, which mentions games between the two countries.

Although the English always claim to be the inventors of football, it's just possible that the game first 'came home' when it was brought to these shores by the Romans. The Greeks and Romans both played games similar to soccer but where the ball could be carried – the Greek game was called *episkyros*, the Roman *harpastum* – and invading Roman legions may well have brought it with them. Legend has it that a home team beat a legionary side in a famous victory in AD 276, a result which must rank alongside non-league Hereford's victory over Newcastle in the 1972 FA Cup third round as one of the great upsets.

These games weren't exactly what you would call tactically astute. Witnessing such a thing as passing the ball was about as likely as seeing a tackle which didn't involve twenty people. We're talking about mass brawls with a ball which would make the Wimbledon side of the mid-1980s look like a bunch of ballet dancers. In the chaotic village melees which ensued up and down Britain, from which soccer and rugby both eventually emerged, a round or oval object – often an inflated pig's bladder – was kicked, punched or carried towards goal. Releasing the ball was seen as an act of cowardice so if you got hold of it you ran until you lost it, something which usually involved a fair amount of pain and possibly a broken limb or worse. Never mind an early bath, avoiding an early grave was challenge enough.

Nevertheless, in an age where gory public executions and witch burnings were the light entertainment of the day, 'football' increased in popularity and games were played more and more often, and not just on festival days. Starting with King Edward in 1314 a succession of kings tried to ban it, worried that it was creating civil disorder and distracting the peasants from their work. In 1365 King Edward III tried to prohibit the game because his soldiers preferred it to fighting and Richard II issued a proclamation in 1389 complaining that it interfered with archery practice.

Queen Elizabeth I, too, condemned the sport which contemporary writer, Sir Thomas Elyot, denounced as 'a pastime to be utterly objected by noble men, the game giving no pleasure, but beastlie furie and violence'. By now huge games of mob football involving up to 500 people were taking place in London, notably at Smithfield, Cheapside and The Strand. The hugely violent conflicts often lasted for the entire day and by the end there would be numerous broken bones and, more often than not, a death or two. In the provinces the games were even bigger. The traditional Shrove Tuesday matches in places like Derby and Nottingham were played over the length of the town and a 1602 survey of Cornwall records that the goals for a match were three or four miles apart with groups of two or three parishes uniting to play one another.

By the nineteenth century, however, football – like society – had become slightly more civilised and the game had evolved into something which would be slightly more recognisable to you or I. Still notable for its ferocious tackling and a certain amount of legal handling of the ball, the game was now played on a pitch with two goals about eighty to hundred yards apart and between two teams of equal numbers. The ball consisted of a leather-cased inflated bladder and the object was simply to drive it through your opponents' goal.

When the first eleven-a-side matches were played in the mid-1800s the standard formation was nine forwards and two defenders (known as 'behinds'). Some ultra-defensive sides consisted of a goalkeeper, who wore the same garb as the others and couldn't touch the ball with his hands, a goal 'cover' (a kind of early sweeper), a back and eight forwards. These forwards relied almost entirely on mass dribbling and charging, each expected to dribble past man after man until he scored or lost the ball. His colleagues surrounded him as he made his run, hoping to pick up the ball if he was tackled and so continue the forward momentum.

Initially the sport of peasants and ruffians, by this time football in England had been adopted by the upper classes and most games took place at and between famous public schools like Eton and Harrow. The problem with this was that each school had its own set of rules. The goalposts at Harrow, for instance, were 150 yards apart – the clear forerunner to the rugby try-line – and it was only at Cheltenham that the goals had a crossbar. So when Rugby School pupil William Webb Ellis got fed up during a game of football in 1823 and picked up the ball and began to run with it – instantly inventing the game of rugby – it became clear that a set of defining rules had to be laid down.

Football and rugby officially split at a meeting at the Freemasons' Tavern in Great Queen Street, London in 1863, and the newly formed Football Association produced its first set of rules on 8 December that year. Much of what was decided that day has survived in the modern game – teams of eleven players, matches lasting ninety minutes and goals eighty yards apart – but in many ways the football played then is totally alien to the modern game.

Players, for instance, were not allowed to pick the ball up or throw it to one another, but they were allowed to catch it. As in modern rugby union, if a player caught the ball and made a mark with his heel he was entitled to a free kick. Tripping and hacking was outlawed but if a team touched the ball down rugby-style after it had travelled beyond their opponents' goal line they were entitled to a free kick at goal. Even more rugby-like was the rule that stated that all attacking players ahead of the ball were deemed offside – in other words, all passing had to be backwards.

The tactical nature of football at this time was purely and simply to try and dribble the ball past your opponent in order to gain ground. The offside rule made this inevitable – it was the only way to go forward. And even if passing had been practical, no one did it because it was seen as an admission of inferiority. Consequently, matches were scrappy, untidy affairs.

As the offside rule made defending easier than attacking, formations continued to be top heavy, even when matches became more organised under the new FA rules. The most popular post-1863 formation featured a goalkeeper, two backs (out-and-out defenders), two half backs (essentially midfielders) and six forwards (figure 1). The strikers would all pile forward together, knowing they would have their work cut out to get past the opposition's back two.

During the Football Association's early years alterations to the rules were frequent but slowly and surely the rugby-style laws were phased out. The most important change came with the introduction of the new offside law in 1866, which stated that a player was only offside if there were fewer than three opposition players (including

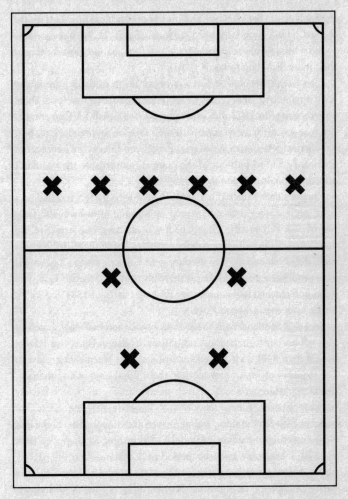

Figure 1: The most popular post-1863 formation, featuring six forwards, two half backs and two backs

the goalkeeper) between him and his opponents' goal line. This meant the ball could now be passed forward (figure 2). However, teams found it hard to adjust to passing the ball forward and most continued their mass dribbling towards goal.

The tactical revolution actually began north of the border where Scottish amateur side Queen's Park were the first to develop a short passing game. In 1872 they entered the first English FA Cup competition and surprised everyone with their style of passing the ball. But, having drawn 0–0 with Wanderers in the semi-final at the Kennington Oval, they had to pull out of the competition because they couldn't afford to stay in London for the replay.

Queen's Park are credited as the first side to perfect football as a team game, rather than one played by a group of individuals. They played a skilled passing game which was effective and attractive. By manoeuvring the ball around defences instead of trying to dribble past them they dramatically increased the speed of their attacks and scored more and more goals. All in all the club won the Scottish Cup nine times and reached two consecutive FA Cup Finals, in 1884 and 1885, losing both to Blackburn Rovers.

In 1873 Scotland won the second official international match in football history (against England, the match the previous year having been drawn 0–0) with a team featuring seven Queen's Park players. The Scots won 4–2, bewildering their opponents with accurate, defence-splitting passes. Scotland, thanks mainly to their relatively intricate passing game, went on to dominate the first decade of matches between the sides, winning seven and drawing two of the first eleven meetings including a famous 7–2 thrashing at Hampden Park in 1878. It was only after this period of dominance that the passing philosophy was finally accepted south of the border and even this was partly because of an influx of Scottish players into English sides. Personally, I think they should have stayed at home and kept it to themselves, but then I'm biased, aren't I?

With the game becoming more sophisticated, teams became more and more aware of the importance of defence and, around 1883, the most popular formation was a slightly more cautious 2–3–5 with two full backs (who stayed in defence at all times), three half backs

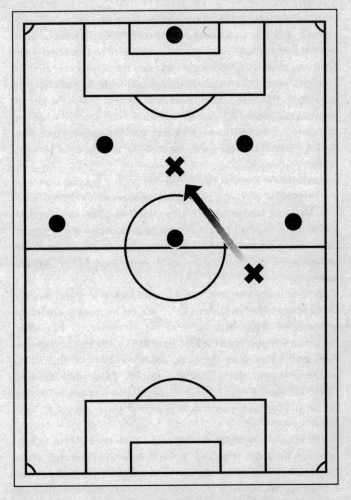

Figure 2: Under the 1866 offside law, attacking players were deemed onside if there were three or more defensive players (including the goalkeeper) between them and the goal line

(essentially defensive midfielders) and five forwards (figure 3). Teams gradually began to understand that throwing half their team forward in a big group was leaving them far too exposed to counter-attacks. The basis of the 2–3–5 formation was that the players kept to their positions, forming an upside down pyramid with the goalkeeper at the bottom. The centre half (the central midfielder) was the crucial player in the system, marking the opposing centre forward when the other side had the ball but when his team gained possession becoming the key playmaker in the team, essentially he was the pivot between defence and attack.

English First Division side Preston North End became known as the 'Invincibles' playing a 2–3–5 formation, becoming the first team to achieve the League and FA Cup double in 1889, the very first season of the Football League. As well as combining a skilful passing game with solid and organised defending, Preston put the emphasis on teamwork and the training of ex-army man Major William Suddell.

By now teams were aware that to earn success they had to train hard and work hard and, after 1883, it was the big, professional clubs of the north which won most of the silverware. In fact, after Blackburn Olympic lifted the FA Cup in 1883 it was another eighteen years until a team from the south, Tottenham Hotspur (then still a Southern League club) lifted the trophy. Teams like Preston, Blackburn Rovers and Aston Villa dominated football by adding precise passing and dramatically improved player fitness to their game.

For many years British football teams persevered almost universally with the 2–3–5 formation. It was elsewhere in the world, where the game had now taken hold, that more imaginative formations and systems began to emerge. The most popular of these was called the 'Method' or 'MM' and was particularly popular in Italy. The 'MM' formation featured two backs, two wing halfbacks and a centre half to make up the first 'M' in front of the goalkeeper and then two wing halfs on either side of three forwards to form the second 'M' (figure 4). Teams would move the ball with quick, short passes along the lines of the 'M's to progress towards goal.

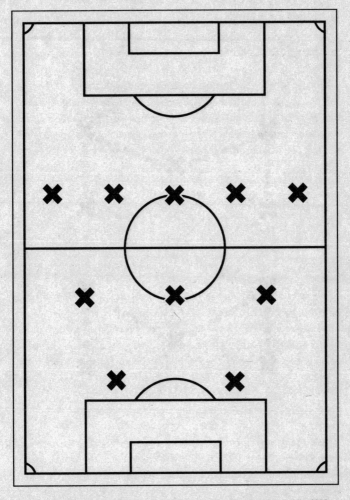

Figure 3: The 2–3–5 formation, popular in British football between the 1880s and the 1920s

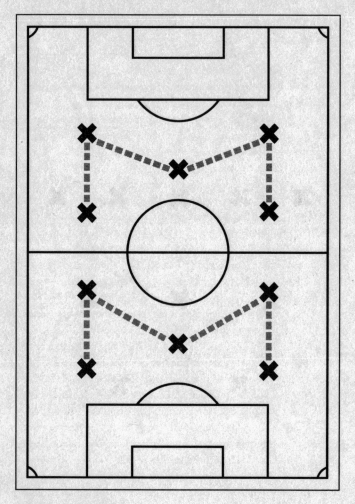

Figure 4: The 'MM' formation

As well as new formations, the new hotbeds of football around the world began to inject new styles of play and tactical philosophies into football. In 1924 Uruguay won the Olympics playing football the like of which no one outside South America had ever imagined. The team combined individual flair, creativity and fantasy with precise passing and quick, incisive attacking movements. It is a style for which South American teams are still known. Uruguay and their near neighbours and arch rivals Argentina played a game as far from the rigid European style as you could get.

British football, however, remained true to character, continuing to be very much set in its ways. It wasn't until 1925 that British teams began to tinker with the good old 2–3–5 formation at all. Even this tinkering was enforced by a change in the offside law, rather than by any tactical ambition.

On 12 June 1925, after a proposal from the Scottish Federation, the offside law was changed so that only two – instead of three – opposition players (including the goalkeeper) had to be between the furthest forward attacking player and the opposition goal line to play him onside (figure 5). The problem with the old law was that teams were able to foil entire attacks simply by pushing up one defender at the right moment (figure 6). Teams like Newcastle were adept at doing this, with one defender pushing right up and one dropping back as cover should the trap be sprung. Under the new law, if the last defender stepped up at the wrong moment and failed to catch the last attacker offside, the attacking team would be clean through on goal.

Before the rule change things had got so bad that play in most matches was becoming squeezed into a narrow strip covering about forty yards in the middle of the field. The offside trap was so easy to execute that defenders were pushing right upfield (figure 7). Newcastle United were the acknowledged masters of this tactic with their backs Bill McCracken and Frank Hudspeth the best oiled offside machine in football. The pair became so identified with the ploy that, legend has it, when one team arrived at Newcastle Central station and the guard blew his whistle the team's centre forward quipped: 'Blimey, offside already!'

It was quite common for games to be interrupted up to forty times

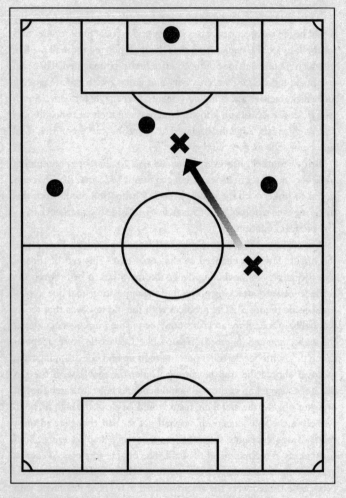

Figure 5: After June 1925 attacking players were onside when there were two, not three, defensive players (including the goalkeeper) between them and the goal line

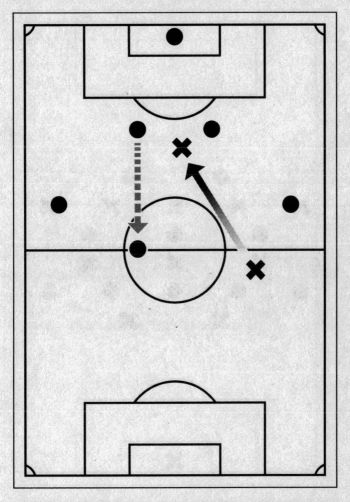

Figure 6: Under the original offside law it was easy to catch attacking players offside by pushing one defender right up the pitch

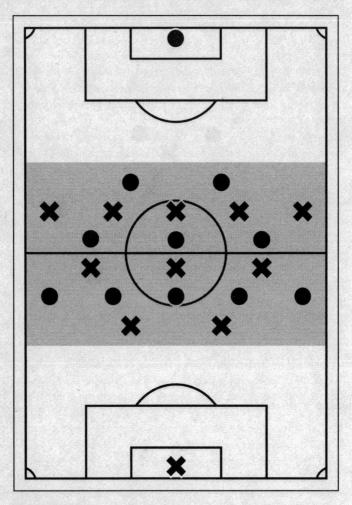

Figure 7: With offside so easy to play, defenders from both teams pushed right up and the game was often squeezed into a very small area

for offside decisions and on at least one occasion infuriated fans invaded the pitch to vent their anger. In response, the FA ran a series of experimental friendlies in which the options considered included adding a forty-yard line to reduce the area in which the offside rule applied or reducing the number of opponents needed to keep a player offside from three to two. They eventually plumped for the latter.

During the following season, 1925/26, the game experienced its biggest revolution since the advent of the passing game in the 1870s. Forwards suddenly had acres of space because defences, now nervous of pushing up to play offside because it was so much more dangerous, had to sit back and wait for them to attack. The game didn't necessarily become better to watch – because defences were so much more nervous the goals they gave away were often the result of mistakes and bad play rather than brilliant attacking movements – but the number of goals scored did increase dramatically. Fans witnessed a third more bulges in the onion bag during the 1925/26 season than they had in the previous campaign.

At first, teams persevered with 2–3–5. It wasn't until legendary Arsenal manager Herbert Chapman realised he had to change something to cope with opposition attackers' new-found freedom that anything changed. After seeing his side lose 7–0 away to Newcastle on 6 October 1925, Chapman immediately sat down for a tactical re-think with club captain Charles Buchan. The pair realised that they had to find a way of blocking the middle of the defence which, in a 2–3–5 formation, simply couldn't cope with five marauding forwards coming at them under the new rules.

Finally, one or the other – accounts vary as to whether it was Chapman or Buchan – suggested that the centre half, who had previously been the midfield general, should drop back to perform a purely defensive role as a stopper. This stopper would be a player whose only real reason for being on the pitch was to stop attackers by heading, tackling and hoofing the ball clear. Then, to make up for the lack of a pivotal player in midfield, two of the five forwards would drop back to supply the creative link between defence and midfield. The result was the 'WM' formation, a system which would go on to provide the basis of football in Britain and much of the rest of the world for the next twenty-five years (figure 8).

Chapman had first revealed the 'WM' brainchild two days after the defeat by Newcastle. Arsenal beat West Ham 4–0 at Upton Park, using Jack Butler as a stop-gap centre half, plugging the gaping holes in defence which had been so apparent at Newcastle just forty-eight hours earlier. However, in December 1926 Chapman unearthed the perfect player for the centre-half position, 'Policeman' Herbie Roberts. A huge, rugged man, Roberts was the archetypal centre half. There wasn't much style or panache about him, but if you wanted the ball headed or hoofed into row Z he was your man. Roberts policed the middle of the defence (hence the nickname) while full backs Charlie Male and Eddie Hapgood responded to the immediate point of attack. If the ball was coming down the left, Hapgood closed down in the area of the ball while Male provided cover in the centre and vice versa when the ball was played down the right (figure 9).

Ahead of the defence the half backs and inside forwards (as they were known in those days) formed a midfield rectangle with, ahead of them, two wingers (wide men whose job it was to cross the ball into the box) and a centre forward. The system had the perfect balance. 'WM' was solid enough at the back but still offered multiple attacking options. Arsenal won the league title in 1931, 1933, 1934, 1935 and 1938 playing this system and the Gunners provided seven of the England team which famously defeated world champions Italy 3–2 at Highbury in 1934. Though for years many match programmes continued to list players in the old 2–3–5 formation, 'WM' formed the basis of play in the domestic game for the next quarter of a century and English football sat back, cockily convinced that no one could teach it anything.

The key role in 'WM' was again the central midfield position and much of Arsenal's success with the system was down to the creative play of Alex James, whom Chapman signed from Preston North End in the summer of 1929. Now that the gap between midfield and attack was so much wider – because defences were sitting back on the edge of their own penalty box not trying to play offside – teams needed a player who could act as the link between defence and attack. By

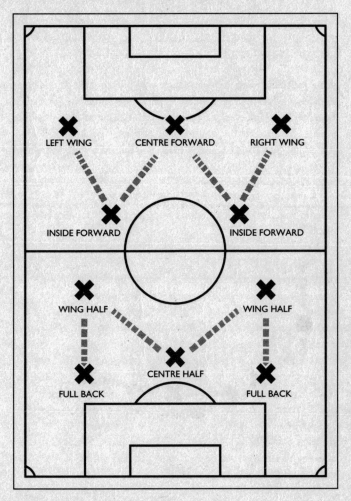

Figure 8: The 'WM' formation

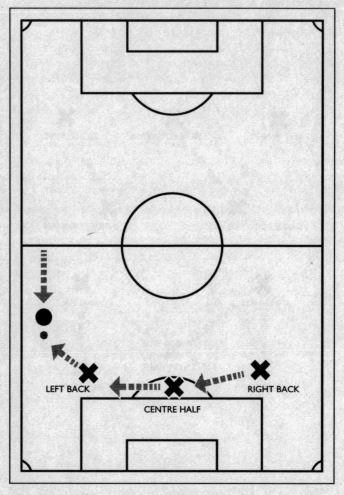

Figure 9: How the defence in a 'WM' formation worked when the ball was coming down the left flank

spraying long, accurate passes to his wingers and centre forward after receiving the ball from defence James made Chapman's system work.

That was the thing about football throughout the years up until, say, the 1950s and 1960s – systems and tactics were important but not nearly as important as they are today. After the 1925 change in the offside law there was so much space on a football field that, whatever the formation, the good players had space in which to play. In the modern game, with its offside traps and pressing midfields, it is much easier for teams to cramp the good players' space and so minimise their influence. Nowadays a team can be beaten even though they have better players than their opponents, simply because they have lost the tactical battle. In the 1920s, 1930s and 1940s that happened less often. The good players had the space in which to exert their authority and so it was the teams with the best players that usually won.

Take Herbert Chapman's Arsenal. They were the first to play with a 'WM' system but it wasn't long before most of their opponents' responded in kind. But Arsenal had Eddie Hapgood, Alex James and great goalscorers like Cliff Bastin and Ted Drake. That's why they won so many league titles. The tactics helped, but the secret of their success was the quality of the players who lined up in that system.

There were exceptions, of course – like the great Austrian 'Wunderteam' which played with an attacking old-style centre half in an 'MM' formation to reach the semi-finals of the 1934 World Cup – but for many years almost every football team in the world played 'WM'.

As we will see in the next few chapters, however, during the 1950s and 1960s tactical thinking on formations and systems became more and more sophisticated and more and more of an influence on the game of football.

CHAPTER 2

Hungary 1953

ENGLAND 3 HUNGARY 6
25 November 1953 (Friendly)
Wembley Stadium. Attendance: 100,000.

Hungary: (2–6–2)

Grosics

Buzansky   Lantos

Bozsik   Lorant   Zakarias

Kocsis   Hidegkuti   Puskas

Budai   Czibor

England: Merrick, Ramsey, Eckersley, Wright, Johnston, Dickinson, Matthews, Taylor, Mortensen, Sewell, Robb

England had never been beaten by foreign opposition at Wembley, but when it finally happened, it happened in style. It only took Hungary a minute to give the home side a taste of what the next eighty-nine would be like, Nandor Hidegkuti swerving skilfully and firing past Merrick in the England goal from twenty yards to make it 1–0. England's equaliser twelve minutes later – Harry Sewell slotting the ball past Grosics from close range against the run of play – seemed to have stemmed the tide but three Hungarian goals in seven first-half minutes stunned the Wembley crowd. The last of these, scored by Puskas, who dragged the ball back with his studs and then fired into the top corner from a narrow angle, is one of the best goals ever to grace the hallowed turf. Despite fielding a side which included Stanley Matthews, Billy Wright and legendary striker Stan Mortensen, England simply weren't at the races. At half-time it was 4–2 to the Hungarians and there was no way back for England. In the second half Alf Ramsey converted a penalty for England but Hungary scored two more, Hidegkuti completing his hat-trick, to make the scoreline a thoroughly historic one.

'Look at that little fat chap there,' one England player is said to have chuckled to his team-mates as they lined up in the Wembley tunnel before running out to face Hungary. 'We'll murder this lot.' Whoever that England player was he should have kept his mouth shut. For the player he was referring to was Hungarian captain Ferenc Puskas – a man whose portly physique certainly gave no clues as to his ability to perform miracles with a football. Over the next ninety minutes Puskas orchestrated the total and utter destruction of an England side considered then (by themselves at least) to be the best in the world.

This famous defeat by the team that was to become known as the 'Magnificent Magyars' was the first time England had ever lost to non-British opposition at Wembley. Their only other defeat on home soil had been at Goodison Park in 1949 by an Ireland team who had included nine players from the English Football League. Austria had come close at Wembley in 1951 when Alf Ramsey equalised late in the game from the penalty spot and in October 1953, just a month or so before the visit of Hungary, another late penalty from Ramsey had earned a 4–4 draw with a FIFA 'Rest of the World' team. The cracks had been appearing in the Wembley fortifications, but no one could have foreseen this heavy defeat. Or could they?

In fact England's blinkered attitude to world football – they didn't deign to enter the World Cup until 1950 – meant that despite being unbeaten in four years and having won the Olympic gold medal in 1952 the Hungarians arrived at Wembley almost completely unheralded. People simply didn't know how good they were. No one (except, of course, Scotland and very occasionally, Wales) beat England at Wembley. It simply didn't happen. When it did, the country entered a state of shock.

Such was the brilliance of the visitors and so inspired was their strategy that one English football writer was compelled to describe their performance as 'Football dressed in new colours'. Their revolutionary system was devised by coach Gustav Sebes. In an era where every team played the same way, where the 'WM' formation was considered the only conceivable way to play the game, Sebes came up with something new. But the massive shockwaves that his team sent through world football were as much down to the rigidity of football thinking everywhere else as they were to the brilliance of his plan.

What Sebes did, essentially, was to create a new position. Nandor Hidegkuti played with the number nine on his back but that's about as close as he ever got to being a centre forward in this team. What a traditional English centre forward would have done, indeed, what England number nine Stan Mortensen did at the other end, was to go and stand up beside the opposition defence for the whole game. He was the furthest man forward at all times. In reality Hidegkuti was not a centre forward at all, he was an attacking midfielder.

The idea was that instead of the inside forwards Kocsis and Puskas providing passes for the centre forward, Hidegkuti would drop deep and feed them with passes as they pushed forward (figure 10). This would have one of two effects. If the centre half, who traditionally would have marked the centre forward wherever he went, knowing he would always push right forward (figure 11), stuck with him then he would be pulled here, there and everywhere, leaving a gaping hole in the defence for Puskas and Kocsis to exploit. If the centre half, not normally expected to move far from the edge of his penalty area, left Hidegkuti to roam in midfield he would have acres of space in which to carve out opportunities for his team-mates.

Against England the plan worked perfectly. Centre half Harry Johnston was flummoxed. A man who in every game he had ever played in that position would, up until that November day, have been glued to whoever was wearing the number nine shirt, Johnston was suddenly unsure whether to follow Hidegkuti into midfield or to hold his position in the centre of the defence. More often than not he was caught in no man's land doing neither of these things (after the game

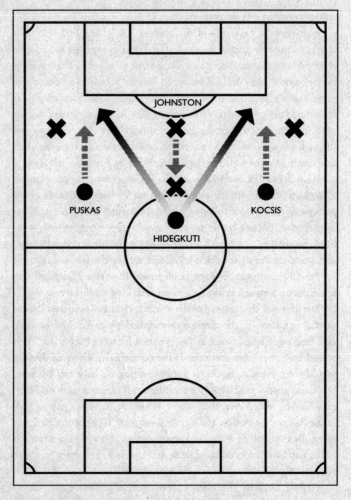

Figure 10: By dropping deep and drawing Johnston out of position, Hidegkuti created gaps in the England defence for Puskas and Kocsis to exploit

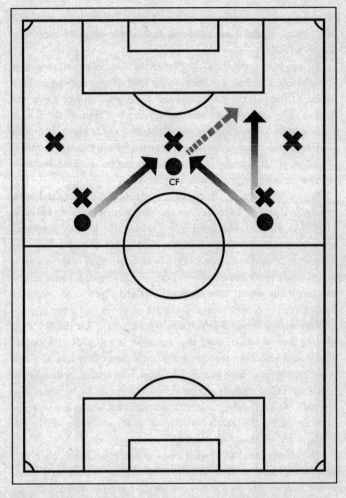

Figure 11: How a traditional English centre forward like Stan Mortensen would play in a 'WM' formation, pushed right up against the opposition centre half

he complained 'I had no one to mark') while full backs Ramsey and Bill Eckersley held their positions and simply played Puskas and Kocsis onside.

To add to the confusion, the Hungarian wingers played very deep – much nearer the halfway line than the English wingers – where they joined in the play in midfield rather than just charging down the flanks. These tactics, allied with near-perfect ball control, short, neat passing and some quite phenomenal shooting made Hungary practically invincible. And the result on that fateful afternoon was that a crowd of 100,000 people plus another eleven on the pitch in white shirts were completely and utterly stunned.

Even a simple thing like the shirt numbers had the England team at sixes and sevens. Here was a player with number nine on his back playing in midfield. The number five shirt in the English game was always worn by the centre half, but the Hungarian centre half was wearing number three. Number three was supposed to be the left back and what on earth was number five doing in midfield? It sounds crazy but this really would have confused England. Even in my day you looked at players who played in certain numbers and if the opposition tried something different you would say, 'Why the hell's he playing there if he's wearing that number?' In the 1950s the confusion would have been even greater. Number five in the English game would always have been a central defender, no question, and suddenly here's this fellow cruising around in midfield. Even BBC commentator Kenneth Wolstenholme couldn't work out what was going on from high up on the TV gantry so can you imagine what it did to the England players down on the pitch?

The Hungarians had devised a system which made best use of the space to be found on a football pitch in the 1950s. In those days teams didn't look for offside – it was considered too risky after the change in the offside law in 1925 – which meant that the game was far more stretched. You would have one set of defenders sitting on the edge of their eighteen-yard box and the other set doing exactly the same, leaving a much bigger gap between the halfway line and the defence than you would see in the modern game (figure 12). The Hungarian system made maximum use of this area. Instead of pushing their

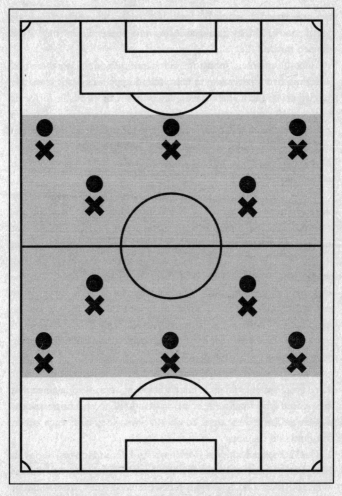

Figure 12: After the change to the offside law in 1925, defences stopped pushing so far up the pitch which left much more room in which to play the game

forwards right up against the English defenders where they would be tightly marked, they dropped back into space where they were allowed time on the ball.

Since his marker, Johnston, didn't go with him into this area, Hidegkuti had the freedom to mastermind England's destruction. He roamed around in midfield, swapping passes with the inside forwards Puskas and Kocsis, waiting until an English defender was pulled towards the ball and left a great big hole for one of the three to run into. For vast chunks of the game you had five England defenders marking no one while the Hungarians played around in front of them to their hearts' content.

At the back Hungary played with a fairly typical defence. They played with the 'M' from the 'WM' formation at the back but the front men lined up almost in a 'U' shape (figure 13). That meant that the England defence was suddenly having to deal with people running at them with the ball and not just from wide areas. Normally the only people who would have run at them at all would have been the wingers, but the England defenders were faced with three centre forwards running at them all at once. One minute they would be standing there with no one to mark, then suddenly Puskas, Hidegkuti and Kocsis would be running at them together from midfield, passing their way past static defenders.

It has to be said, though, that these three were magical players. It was a great system and great tactics but they were all so talented that they would have made almost any system look good. The movement was incredible. They were constantly switching with each other, constantly on the move.

Unlike England, there was nothing rigid about Hungary's play. If Hidegkuti wanted to be the furthest back then he was, and Puskas would push on a bit. The English defence never knew who would be coming at them next.

The remarkable thing about this match if you look at it now is that Hidegkuti constantly picks up the ball in the centre circle just inside his own half. All three of them, Hidegkuti, Puskas and Kocsis were more than happy to come into their own half to receive the ball and build up an attack. But at that time it was unheard of to see a player

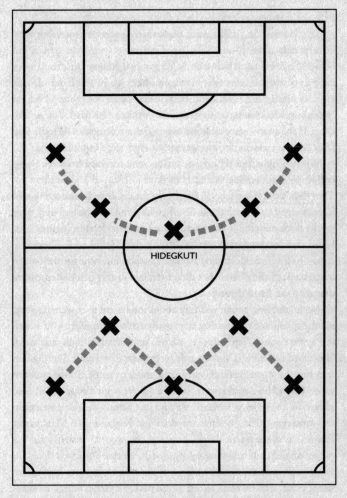

Figure 13: Hungary's 'UM' formation with Hidegkuti withdrawn into midfield

with the number nine on his back in his own half.

The Hungarian tactics were not exactly rocket science, but they were totally alien to anything the England players had ever faced before. England wing halves Billy Wright and Jimmy Dickinson were used to playing against two players in that area just in front of their own defence, but suddenly they were faced by three because Hidegkuti was coming so deep to join Puskas and Kocsis. And so the three Hungarians were able to avoid the attentions of Wright and Dickinson by passing it through them. They were outnumbered.

When Wright and Jimmy Dickinson went forward from the wing-half areas, Puskas, Kocsis and Hidegkuti just stayed and let them go. They didn't chase them back. Normally the inside right and left would have charged back with them. So when England lost the ball they were totally outnumbered in the area in front of their defence (figures 14a, b and c). The Hungarians certainly took risks in this way. They were happy to leave the defending to their defence and wait for the ball to come back to them, and that did cost them in this game. Remember that they did let in three goals.

No matter how much you talk about the system they were playing, it's the quality of the passing that really strikes you when you watch the game again. The play is of an unbelievably high standard. Hidegkuti played in a similar role to the one that Teddy Sheringham and Eric Cantona have played in the modern game. In the modern game Hidegkuti would have been a player who dropped off and played in 'the hole', a forward playing just behind the main striker in the same way that Sheringham does for England and Manchester United. In the modern game, however, he would normally have a player ahead of him. Hungary rotated it, so that Puskas, Hidegkuti and Kocsis took turns to be ahead of the play. And there were times when none of them were ahead of the play, all three coming forward around the ball. It's almost as if they had a front line of Teddy Sheringham, Eric Cantona and Paul Scholes, all interchanging constantly between the centre circle and the penalty spot. There were very few long balls – just crisp, incisive passing.

Puskas's famous goal, Hungary's third, which came halfway through the first half, showed you pretty much everything about the

Figure 14(a)

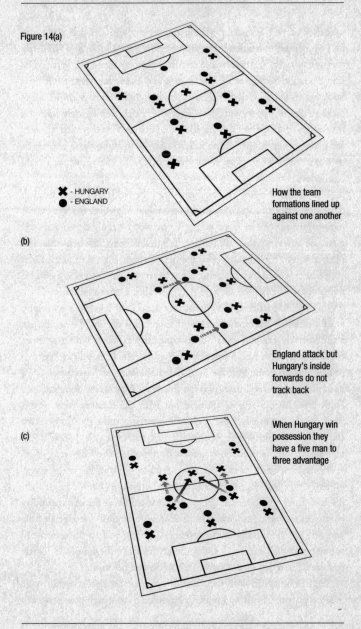

X - HUNGARY
● - ENGLAND

How the team
formations lined up
against one another

(b)

England attack but
Hungary's inside
forwards do not
track back

(c)

When Hungary win
possession they
have a five man to
three advantage

way they played. It said everything about the team. The ball was being played around in midfield, England couldn't get a kick, and suddenly the left winger, Czibor, made a run across to the right wing. The English right back, Ramsey, let him go so Eckersley on the left now had two to mark. Czibor received the ball and played it into Puskas on the edge of the six-yard box after the Hungarian captain had run fifty yards from deep. The England defence had been pulled all over the place – they simply didn't know whether to track these players or to leave them when they went wandering, and the result was total confusion.

But when Puskas received the ball he still had two English defenders in front of him and, seemingly, nowhere to go. What happened next can be summed up in one word – genius. In one movement he received the ball, dragged it back onto his left foot and blasted it into the top corner of the net. That's the kind of tactic most supporters would buy a season ticket to see. So the goal was a combination of well-planned tactical play and sheer, utter brilliance.

In 1955 Manchester City centre forward Don Revie – a man who would one day become manager of England – decided he would try a similar ploy. He played as a deep-lying centre forward in the manner of Hidegkuti with Ken Barnes in the Puskas role. It was an indictment of the English game and the fact that the lessons of November 1953 had not been learned that, playing this way, City threw defences into confusion. By playing in midfield but with the number nine on his back, Revie consistently flummoxed his marker and City reached two successive FA Cup Finals, losing the first to Newcastle 1–3 in 1955 but winning the second 3–1 against Birmingham the following year.

Revie later said: 'If they had bothered to think about it there was no great problem. But players and managers were chained to straight up-and-down attitudes. As the centre forward I was the responsibility of the centre half. And when he attempted to follow me a great hole was left in the middle of the defence. All they had to do was detail someone to pick me up, leaving the centre half where he was, ready to take over when I appeared in an advanced position.'

English football, with tactics so set in concrete that it would take more than one result to break the mould, took many years to even begin to evolve after the Hungarian disaster. Even right after the game the result was considered a freak and was put down to bad defending. The response was not to re-think strategy or try to discover what went wrong – instead many of the players were made into scapegoats. Two men making their international debuts that day, Ernie Taylor of Blackpool and George Robb of Spurs, were never again picked for England.

In 1971 the England players who had played against Hungary in 1953 attended a reunion function to which Ferenc Puskas was also invited. The story goes that Ramsey greeted his fellow full back, Bill Eckersley, with a quizzical, 'Hello, it is Bill isn't it?' Puskas remarked, 'It was like that when they played us – the team hardly seemed to know each other's names.'

Six months after the 6–3 drubbing, England fielded a 'WM' formation for the return match, a friendly in Budapest. This time it was even worse, they lost 7–1. As for the Hungarians, they went from strength to strength. That famous win was part of a thirteen-year unbeaten home run which stretched from 1943 to 1956 and during the 1950s they went twenty-nine games without defeat, home or away. The run was brought to an end only in the 1954 World Cup Final when they were finally beaten 3–2 by a West Germany side they had thrashed 8–3 earlier in the competition. The Hungarians had led 2–0 but, with Puskas playing despite carrying a serious ankle injury, the best team in the world was finally beaten and robbed of the ultimate prize it so richly deserved.

It was to take England thirteen years to erase the memory of that shattering Wembley defeat. After winning the World Cup in 1966, England manager Alf Ramsey – who played at right back on that fateful day in 1953 – said: 'I have had one great ambition hanging over me for years, to replace the image of that great Hungarian side by the image of an even greater England team. From that time everybody has judged football by those wonderful Hungarians.'

CHAPTER 3
Four at the Back

● ●

Four at the back is my system. I can quite happily say that if I ever became a manager I would line up my first team with a flat back four. By that I mean a straight back line across the width of the pitch featuring a left back, two centre backs alongside each other in the middle and a right back. As far as I'm concerned, when it comes to building the solid foundations of a football team, a platform from which to attack, it's the defensive system that – when everything is clicking into place – works best.

Although it seems that there are hundreds of systems and variations of systems in modern football, they are all based on one of two options – either four or five at the back. You can play with three up front like Joe Kinnear's Wimbledon often do or you can play with three in midfield as Alex Ferguson likes Manchester United to do at times, but basically you've got to choose between four or five at the back. Anything that happens ahead of your defensive unit is tweaking the system.

The so-called flat back four was first developed by Brazil, who  unveiled the system during the 1958 World Cup. At a time when most teams were still playing the 'WM' formation with defenders designated to mark specific attackers, the Brazilians came up with the idea of marking zones rather than individuals. So when an attacking player moved from the middle of the goal to his left, rather than the centre back being dragged out of position he would let him go and leave the right back to pick him up. If a forward dropped deep, the defence would let him go and a midfielder would pick him up. The idea was that, with good communication and organisation, the defensive line would always be in place, and it was so successful that it wasn't long before it had been adopted all over the world.

My admiration for playing four at the back comes partly from the fact that all the successful teams that I ever played in used this method. I was brought up with Jim McLean at Dundee United playing the system and throughout my career it was the platform for the success of every team I played for. It's a hugely successful system, and no modern side has won the English league title playing any other way.

Just look at Manchester United. On the few occasions when Alex Ferguson has experimented with five at the back he's had poor results. Just look at the AC Milan side who were winning European Cup after European Cup in the late 1980s and 1990s. Their manager, Arrigo Sacchi, based his whole philosophy on playing four at the back. They dominated football. The current Brazil team, the world champions, are another back four side. I think a lot of people think of four at the back as a prehistoric English system laughed at by the rest of the world; but, in fact, probably the most flamboyant, attacking team in the world uses it and you will see a back four in operation in the Maracana Stadium in Rio just as you might on a freezing cold February night at Gresty Road, Crewe.

A back four is much harder to play than a back five. It means spilling more sweat on the training ground. When you see teams playing with three centre backs in the Premiership, the players usually spend the entire game in place as a three and rarely drift into midfield. A back four, on the other hand, is continually moving. The entire defence must be in constant communication and regimentally organised.

The way I like to explain how it works – or how it should work – is by imagining that the four defenders are attached by a stretch of rope. Now when the ball is with your right back and he goes forward, the rope automatically tugs the other three defenders across the pitch and brings the left back in, close to his centre backs (figures 15a, b and c). Then if the ball gets switched across the pitch to the left-hand side the left back goes to join in, so dragging the rope round and

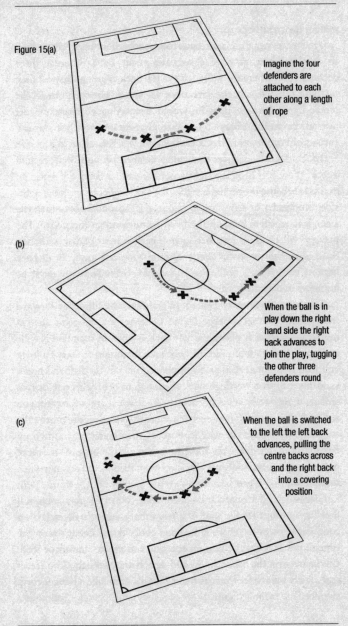

Figure 15(a)

Imagine the four defenders are attached to each other along a length of rope

(b)

When the ball is in play down the right hand side the right back advances to join the play, tugging the other three defenders round

(c)

When the ball is switched to the left the left back advances, pulling the centre backs across and the right back into a covering position pulling the right back in.

That's the way the classic back four works. It's constantly moving so that you always have three back, but it's a different three depending on where the ball is. If the left back is going forward then the right back steps back in to cover. He should never go behind the centre backs because then he would be playing everyone onside; instead, he should always take up a covering position just about a yard ahead of the centre back on the right but very close to him.

Four at the back gives you good balance between defence and attack. If the ball is on the right you have good attacking balance on that side because the right back goes forward and plays with the right-sided midfielder and the inside midfielder. This creates a neat little triangle in which to work the ball and create openings (figure 16). The players will be close together, giving each other options whenever their team has the ball. That's counter-balanced nicely in defence because the left back will come round and cover. They will never be outnumbered at the back.

Think of Manchester United. When Gary Neville goes forward from right back to support David Beckham on the right side of midfield, whoever is playing at left back – whether it be Phil Neville or Dennis Irwin – will hold. He will tuck in alongside Gary Pallister and Ronny Johnsen so that if the opposition win the ball and break suddenly United have three back – enough to deal with one or two strikers. Conversely when his brother or Irwin charges forward, you will find Gary tucked in alongside his centre backs on the other side.

That was always the way it worked when teams played two up front. It varies a little bit sometimes these days because if you're playing a side which only plays one up front then there are times when that piece of rope can become an elastic band. In other words, both full backs can go forward at the same time. When Chelsea are in full flow at Stamford Bridge against a team that's come to defend, it's a common sight to see Graeme Le Saux or Celestine Babayaro on the edge of the opposition's box on one side and Frank Sinclair or Steve Clarke over on the other. In the old days it was a tough old piece of rope, fairly inflexible, whereas these days it's more like a bungee cord, stretched to its limit (figure 17).

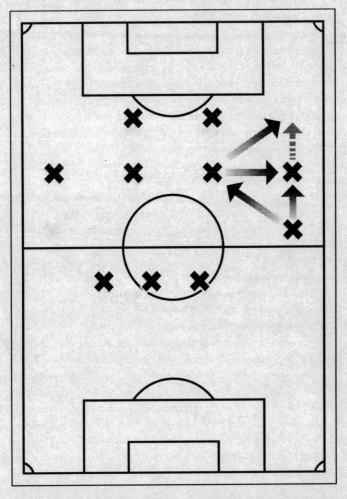

Figure 16: Playing four at the back means that the player on the ball, in this case the right back, usually has team-mates near him with whom to work short, safe passes

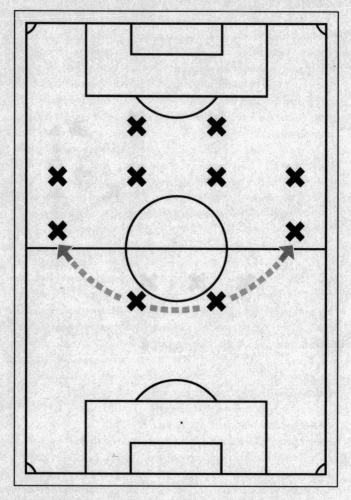

Figure 17: When opposition teams are playing with just one up front, both full backs can go forward at the same time

Usually, however, you'll see a pretty classic back four in the Premiership, with two centre backs and a covering player as your defensive security at all times. Once you have that philosophy working as the basis of your defence you must decide if you are going to be a team that holds the line. Are you going to push your back four up the pitch in a line, letting strikers run through and trying to catch them offside? It's a very profitable way of playing if you get it right, because you can be breaking down your opponents' attacks before they've even started and taking umpteen free kicks from ten yards inside your own half, but you really have to decide whether the players you have at your disposal are vocal enough to do it.

Communication is the secret here. We used to have a problem with Paul McGrath when I was assistant manager to Ron Atkinson at Aston Villa in the early 1990s. Paul really was a wonderful player, a truly magnificent defender, but it used to be a nightmare for us because Ron Atkinson and I wanted the back four to hold. We wanted to hold up and catch people offside. But Paul was very quiet. He didn't talk a lot on the pitch and without communication it's impossible to set an offside trap. He was such a fantastic player but he never, ever played offside. It just didn't seem natural to him. He was a player who wanted to defend every ball. The result was that we hardly ever got an offside and we ended up having to come to terms with the fact that we just couldn't play that way and that if we wanted Paul in the team, which we did, we had to play a different way (figures 18a and b).

It was hard because we ended up defending every attack. We knew that if a forward made a run, Paul would go with him, whereas in a perfect world if a forward makes a straight run you stand your ground as a line and know that if he runs past you he will be offside. So you let him make senseless runs and you get offsides and free kicks.

Playing a successful and efficient back four requires different kinds of players to those who might make up a back five. When it comes to the full backs the first thing that you look for is a good defender. Anything you get at the other end is a bonus. You look for someone like Gary Neville or Stuart Pearce or Arsenal's Lee Dixon and Nigel Winterburn. These men are no mugs when it comes to going forward, but their primary strength is their defensive play in their own half.

Figure 18(a)

A back four 'holding the line' stands its ground and allows an opposing forward to run offside

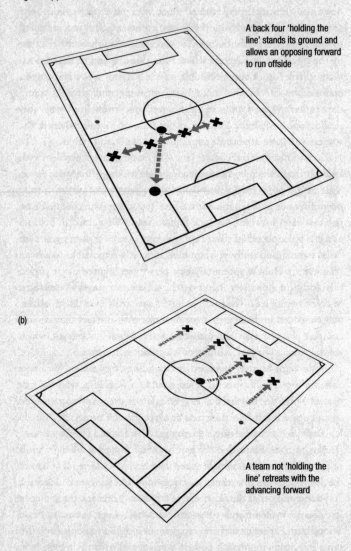

(b)

A team not 'holding the line' retreats with the advancing forward

They can tackle, they can head the ball, they read the game well and it takes some pretty clever play to get past them.

The biggest difference between four at the back and five at the back is that the people who play as wing backs in a five are invariably poorer defenders than the people who play in a four – for example, Jason McAteer at Liverpool and Fernando Nelson at Aston Villa. These men are not natural defenders. But in a four it is vital that your full backs are able to tackle, read the play and sense danger. I remember Graeme Souness saying that not enough players sense danger. This is what natural defenders do. They read the game in a different way to attackers. As a full back in a four you have to make sure that you don't get caught too far forward when the ball is on the other side of the pitch. Otherwise there's a chance you will leave a great big space behind you and if the ball gets played over the top for a nippy striker like Arsenal's Ian Wright or Michael Owen of Liverpool there will be nothing you can do about it.

It is also important that your full backs are good users of the ball. This is because ideally you want the ball with your full back if you can get it to him as essentially he has the whole pitch to aim at. He can hit it long or short. He can play it down the line or chip it in to a front man, he can knock it inside to a midfielder or lay it back to the centre back (figure 19). Your full back needs this kind of range of passing on top of his all-important defensive ability and awareness. If you're really lucky, your full back will also have the extra athleticism and skill to overlap the wide midfielder. When the ball is with the wide midfielder but his route forward is blocked, by running outside him the full back will give him someone to pass to in the perfect position from which to attack the penalty area.

England's Gary Neville is the perfect example of a classic full back. During Euro 96 he played in a fairly standard back four alongside Tony Adams, Gareth Southgate and Stuart Pearce. He wasn't charging forward at every opportunity and leaving gaps at the back. He knew his primary role was to defend, and that it was important to choose his moments to go forward. However, when the right moment did arise, he was able to enter the attack to devastating effect and one such moment transformed England's entire tournament.

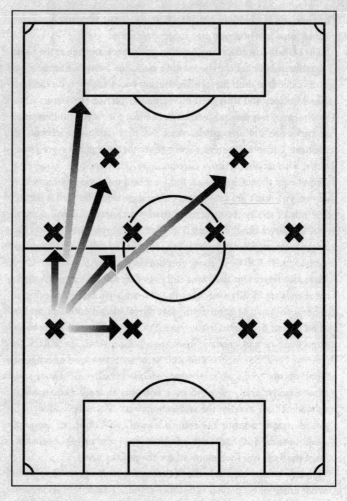

Figure 19: The passing options of a full back

Having drawn 1–1 with Switzerland, Terry Venables' side was struggling in its next game against Scotland. Then early in the second half and with the ball being worked on the right Neville saw a chance to advance. Joining the play midway into the Scottish half he played a neat one-two with Steve McManaman which opened up the opposition defence and then fired in a stunning first-time cross to the back post. The cross was perfect, as was Shearer's finish, and England's tournament was up and running. Although, as a proud Scot, that moment hurt me personally, I could see that it was a perfect piece of full-back play.

When it comes to the kind of player you want playing centre back in a back four, I always say give me a defender who can defend and I'll take him. Anything else is a bonus. Give me a couple of lads who can just get it down and pass it ten yards to the full back, but win every tackle and every header and I'll take those two. I'll take players like Gary Pallister of Manchester United, Tony Adams and Steve Bould of Arsenal and Dave Watson of Everton. They are all big, strong players who can be the rock on which your team is built.

No matter how good your players are, to make four at the back work one of them must be the boss. At Arsenal Tony Adams controls everything. The call for the whole back four to 'stay' (to hold the line where it is), the call to 'step up' (to push up as a line to play the opposing strikers offside) or 'drop off' (to retreat a few steps) comes from him. He is always talking. Communication is probably a word which isn't used enough in football, but it plays such a huge part all over the pitch. Someone like Tony Adams might not have the natural ability of Paul McGrath, but he's worth his weight in gold because of his ability to read the game and communicate.

Communication is a basic thing. Players must constantly tell each other what's going on behind them, where they should be moving, who they should be picking up and when they should be pushing up. On top of that basic communication what you will have if, say, you're defending a setpiece on the edge of the box, is that when your centre back or your captain screams a particular word everyone knows that's the signal to rush out. Most communication, though, is basic, instructional stuff. You might not hear it when you're watching a game on television but players are constantly talking to each other, screaming simple instructions like 'man on' when a player is about to be challenged, 'line ball' when a player wants the ball played along the touchline or 'release' to let him know that he should pass it because he's coming under pressure.

Playing a successful back four is all about familiarity and habit. Just look at the consistency that Arsenal have had in recent times. Adams, Bould, Dixon and Winterburn have provided the granite-like foundations for the Gunners for getting on for ten years now. These players have an almost telepathic understanding. The difference between Arsenal starting the season with these four players in defence and a team who start the season with a new centre back and a new full back is the same as the difference between a golfer who hits sixty balls a day and a golfer who hits 6,000 balls a day. In the same way, a back four which has played forty games together is likely to be better than one with equally good players which has only played fifteen. The fewer injuries you have and the fewer changes you make to your back four, the better it will work as a unit. That's why managers will more often than not use a system right through the club, so that if they do get an injury they can bring someone in from the reserves and he can slot in and do the job. I would be amazed if you found many clubs where the first team plays four at the back and the reserves play five.

I think the reason that many managers in modern football deviate from playing four at the back is because they're not totally confident in the ability of their defenders. They want some insurance. Perhaps that's why when Kenny Dalglish first went to Newcastle he immediately switched the team from playing four at the back to five. He saw how many goals the team had been letting in playing four. He looked at his centre backs, people like Darren Peacock and Phillipe Albert, and thought perhaps that they weren't that strong. He looked at full backs like Warren Barton and John Beresford who aren't pure defenders, but are more like players from the Keegan era whose instinct was always to be bombing forward and getting involved at the other end, and he decided that he had to do something to protect his goal.

Figure 20(a)

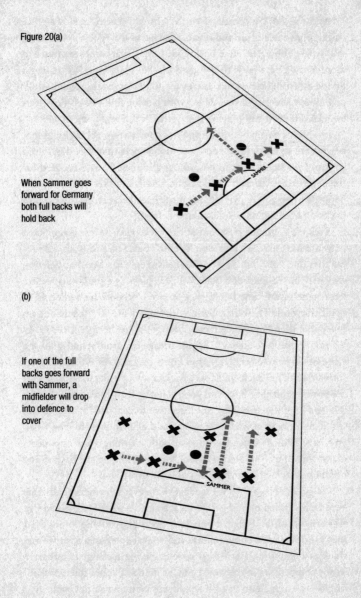

When Sammer goes
forward for Germany
both full backs will
hold back

(b)

If one of the full
backs goes forward
with Sammer, a
midfielder will drop
into defence to
cover

As far as I'm concerned, if you've got two centre backs who you trust and two neat, tidy and reliable full backs then you should never, ever worry about playing a back four. I think that we'll see more and more teams going back to the good old flat back four. We've had a period when managers like Glenn Hoddle, Roy Evans, Ruud Gullit and Arsène Wenger have dabbled with playing five, but of those four only Hoddle was still playing the system at the beginning of 1998.

I think it's partly because managers and coaches are realising that players are so much fitter and more mobile now that they don't need so many defenders back in position at all times. There's no need for three defenders to stay back against one attacker as sometimes happens when you're playing five at the back because the three centre backs do nothing but stay back and defend.

Even the Germans play four at the back. They have a magnificent player in Matthias Sammer who loves to come forward from defence, but they don't play him as a traditional sweeper in a five-man defence; they play him as part of a back four. He plays as a traditional centre back most of the time but with a licence to choose his moments to bomb forward. The other German defenders are so athletic and so quick that they can handle most situations when he goes forward. In relation to the rope analogy, he just breaks free from it and someone else eases in to take his place. They know that as soon as Sammer goes forward both full backs must stay back or a midfielder must drop into his position. So they have still always got at least three back (figures 20a and b). Often they may just leave two to deal with a lone striker. It's all a question of what you want to do with your extra man when you have enough defenders to deal with anything your opponents might throw at you. Do you want him standing at the back doing nothing or do you want him in a positive area?

OK, so I'm biased. All the medals I have ever won in football came with teams which played with a back four. It's what I know and I've seen it work. I think that if you have good players who know what they are doing, who communicate and who are prepared to move and think as a unit, then it's the best system. Put me in charge of any team in any competition in the world and, as long as I've got the right kind of players available to me, I'll be playing with four at the back.

CHAPTER 4
England 1966

● ●

ENGLAND 4 WEST GERMANY 2 (after extra time, full-time
score 2–2)
30 July 1966 (World Cup Final)
Wembley Stadium. Attendance 96,923

England: (4–4–2)

Banks

Cohen   Charlton, J.   Moore   Wilson

Ball   Stiles   Charlton, R.   Peters

Hurst   Hunt

Germany: Tilkowski, Hottges, Schulz, Weber, Schnellinger,
Beckenbauer, Haller, Overath, Seeler, Held, Emmerich

*Bedecked in an unfamiliar red strip which is now synonymous with
English football's finest hour, England took to their home pitch at
Wembley as hot favourites to beat West Germany in the World Cup
Final. You could have heard a pin drop when the Germans scored in
the thirteenth minute. It was the first time England had been behind
in the tournament but they were trailing for only six minutes. After
being tripped by Overath just inside the West German half in the
nineteenth minute, Bobby Moore picked himself up and launched a
quick free kick bang onto the head of Geoff Hurst: 1–1. From then
on England controlled the game, but it wasn't until thirteen minutes*

*from time that they scored again when Martin Peters smacked the ball
home after Hurst's shot had been blocked. Wembley celebrated the
World Cup's winning goal, but then disaster struck. A minute from
time West Germany got a free kick just outside the box. Emmerich
took it and all hell broke loose as it ricocheted around the six-yard
line, before eventually falling to Weber who prodded it home.
England had to start all over again. Ten minutes into extra time Alan
Ball crossed, Geoff Hurst turned and thumped the ball towards goal
and it smashed against the bar, seeming to bounce on the line and
come out. As the England forwards claimed a goal Weber headed
clear. It's still a bone of contention today but when the referee went
to consult his linesman he didn't need to speak Russian to understand
his official's nod of the head. The goal stood. After that the Germans
appeared to lose all heart as well as strength, some people ran on the
pitch and Geoff Hurst made sure there would never be any doubt by
firing in his third to make him the first and only World Cup Final hat-
trick scorer. England had won the World Cup.*

I think 1966 was the first time I ever heard the word 'tactics'.
Everyone was talking about England and their 'wingless wonders'.
Nearly all British teams at this time played with two wingers, players
whose only role on the pitch was to attack. Their job was to hug the
touchline way up the field in their opponents' half and, when they got
the ball, to take on the full back and get a cross into the box. They
didn't have to track back and help out the defence or tackle in
midfield; they were men who would come off the pitch after every
game with chalk from the touchline all over their boots.

Since I was old enough to walk I had watched Rangers playing
4–2–4 with people like Willie Henderson and Davie Wilson as out-
and-out wingers, really going at people and ripping their hearts out.
Scotland had always prided itself on having great wingers – like the
Wembley Wizards who beat England 5–1 at Wembley in 1928 (well,
I had to get them in somewhere didn't I?) – and so it was a massive
shock to sit down in front of the television at home in Glasgow and
watch a team which didn't have a single one win the World Cup. The
fact that the team I watched lift the Jules Rimet trophy was none other

than England only compounded the shock this particular eleven-year-old suffered during those difficult weeks.

The thing about this England team, however, is that although they were 'wingless wonders' they weren't 'widthless wonders'. Alf Ramsey built a side which had such versatility and talent in the midfield that it could create openings from all angles – including wide areas – but it could also provide the sort of strength and defensive cover that a team with two men constantly stranded out on the wing could not.

In Martin Peters, Nobby Stiles, Bobby Charlton and Alan Ball, Ramsey had a group of midfielders whose levels of movement, awareness and skill were so high that he didn't need wingers. But that didn't mean the team didn't have width. If you watch the game you will see Peters running down the left and Alan Ball running down the right. But you will also see them swapping sides, running through the middle and getting back in defence. With a traditional winger, when the other side had possession he was out of the game. He just waited for it to come back to him. But Ramsey's midfielders were never out of it. They were real hard workers. Ball and Peters worked up and down the lines but also in and out. They worked through the middle, they tracked back to defend and they cropped up in the penalty area to score at the other end. They were multi-dimensional players not one-dimensional wingers.

Before the 1966 World Cup Alf Ramsey stated: 'This side can be the greatest that football has ever had, the greatest football will ever know.' That was some boast, but the England manager knew he had the players to win the World Cup and was convinced he had devised a system to ensure that they did just that. It was a system that had first begun to take shape in his mind when he was manager of Ipswich Town in the 1950s.

The popular belief in English football was that Alf Ramsey had achieved a miracle at Portman Road when his team won promotion from the Third Division in his first season in charge (1955/56), reached the First Division four years later and then, incredibly, won the League Championship in 1962. Imagine if someone like Wrexham did that now. It's inconceivable. It was a footballing fairytale and

Ramsey was portrayed as some sort of magician. The future England manager, however, just shrugged his shoulders and later insisted that all he had done was give his opponents tactical problems they had never had to deal with before.

The key element of Ramsey's Ipswich masterplan was to play spindly-legged half back Jimmy Leadbetter on the left wing, not to beat full backs and get dangerous crosses into the box as wingers were expected to in those days but to play long passes forward from deep to eager, powerful attackers on the edge of the box. Opposing full backs would be drawn forward towards Leadbetter, only to find the ball being played over their heads and into acres of space behind them for forwards Ted Phillips and Ray Crawford (figure 21).

It was a tactic that helped Ipswich to the League Championship, but in the 1962 Charity Shield it was rumbled. Ramsey's side were thrashed 5–1 by Spurs after Tottenham boss Bill Nicholson instructed his right back, Ted Baker, not to be drawn upfield and ordered his midfielders to pick up Leadbetter while Baker and left back Ron Henry marked Crawford and Phillips. This left centre half Maurice Norman to clean up (figure 22). Although this ploy stifled Ramsey's system he had already won the league and within a matter of months he was appointed manager of England.

From his appointment in October 1962 Ramsey flirted with the basic principles of 4–2–4 with two out-and-out wingers but he was never convinced it could win him the World Cup. History was against his change of tactics, since England had still only lost four times on home soil against non-British opposition in their entire history playing that way, but Ramsey realised that football was changing. Teams were becoming quicker, stronger and better organised and he was adamant that defence would be the key to the World Cup and that he simply could not afford two wingers who gave nothing to the team when they lost possession. He wanted midfielders with mobility who could run all day and contribute at both ends of the pitch.

On 8 December 1965 Ramsey revealed his creation to the world. Having fielded an increasingly successful team based on midfield strength and earned away wins in Germany and Sweden the previous summer, he decided to play a 'wingless' 4–4–2 formation for the first

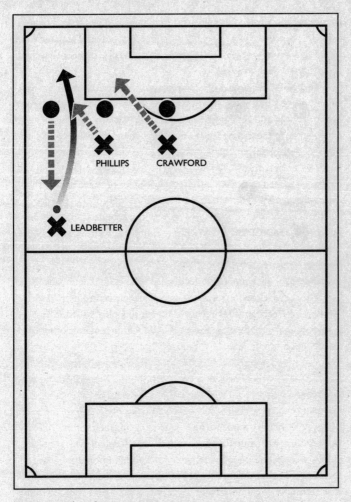

Figure 21: Ramsey's highly successful tactic with Ipswich Town. Left winger Jimmy Leadbetter stays deep, drawing the opposition full back towards him and creating space for Phillips and Crawford to run into as the ball is played long

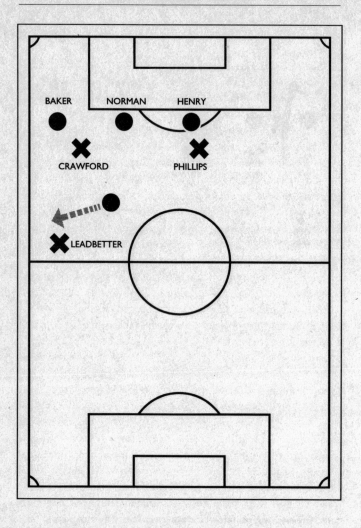

Figure 22: Bill Nicholson's Spurs side countered the tactic by detailing a midfield player to challenge Leadbetter, leaving the defence intact

time, against Spain in Madrid. Publicly labelled 4–3–3 by the media to whom this system was as alien as it was to England's opponents, the formation featured a traditional back four. Ramsey picked a midfield of George Eastham, Nobby Stiles and Bobby Charlton through the middle with Alan Ball constantly switching sides and a forward line of Baker and Hunt.

Nobby Stiles swept up in front of the back four but the other three midfielders were given licence to support the front two, interchanging as they saw fit. It worked a treat. Spanish full backs Reija and Sanchis didn't know who to mark and as the rest of the Spanish team tried desperately to work out what was happening, the English midfield ran the show. Ramsey's side won 2–0. Two months later this new formation, based on midfield movement and aggression, triumphed over West Germany in a less convincing Wembley friendly and, in April, the side won 4–3 against Scotland at Hampden Park. Ramsey was very confident and on the eve of the first game of the tournament he famously declared: 'England will win the 1966 World Cup.'

And, of course, that's exactly what they did. Ramsey, however, didn't go completely wingless in the group stages of the tournament. In the first game (an unconvincing 0–0 draw with Uruguay) he played Liverpool's John Connelly on the left wing and in the second (a hard earned 2–0 win over Mexico) he played Terry Paine on the right. Against France in the final group game he used his third winger, Ian Callaghan of Liverpool, as the team strove to find any sort of consistency. Another 2–0 win followed, but it was only in the quarter-final against Argentina that the manager finally dropped his one winger strategy, bringing in Alan Ball for Callaghan. He had to do something to boost England's faltering progress against the highly rated Argentinians, but he was also forced to replace goalscoring legend Jimmy Greaves with the more workmanlike Geoff Hurst of West Ham. Greaves was suffering from a shin injury so the switch was enforced, but the team that played against Argentina was so successful that Greaves played no further part in the tournament, much to the Tottenham star's bitter disgust. England beat Argentina 1–0 before defeating Eusebio's Portugal 2–1 in the semi-final to gain the honour of playing West Germany in the final. By winning the trophy with this wingless team, Ramsey's controversial selections were vindicated.

The defence in that now famous team which faced the West Germans played as a straightforward back four. The team had two traditional full backs in George Cohen and Ray Wilson, who were primarily defenders but who were both very comfortable going forward. It was because they didn't have traditional wingers in front of them that they had to have the ability to get forward and get involved in the attack. That was vital for the success of the system. In central defence they had big Jack Charlton and Bobby Moore. Jack was Jack, he was a marker, he headed the ball away, he tackled and defended. Bobby was not a sweeper as such but he was the more cultured footballer. He could defend and he could tackle but his game was all about timing. He would intercept and bring the ball away. People say that modern teams must have defenders who can step out and bring the ball out of defence; he was doing it thirty years ago. He was big enough, brave enough and confident enough to bring the ball forward into midfield and influence the play.

But, as I have said, the big difference was in midfield. In the middle of the park Nobby Stiles and Bobby Charlton were the central players with Stiles sitting in front of the back four. The two wide men were Martin Peters and Alan Ball, but whereas traditional wingers played out wide and stayed out wide, they played tucked infield. If they had to provide width as England went forward then they would do so, pushing out onto the touchline to receive the ball. But when possession was lost they tucked in and made it tight in midfield. It meant that England always had two banks of four, the defence and midfield, lined up as protection when the Germans had the ball.

All four England midfielders were given the freedom when they had the ball to play anywhere on the pitch. Although they had basic positions they had licence to switch with each other at will and they did so constantly. The movement in the team was stupendous. During the game Martin Peters would realise, for instance, that there was no point in him going down the left because Alan Ball had already gone there, so he would switch and go down the right. Then when England lost the ball he would drop in on the right to defend. Ball, meanwhile, would stay on the left, until such time as it was appropriate to change back. It was all about a group of players with an incredible under-standing of each other being given the freedom to play their natural game.

A lot of teams at this time played in straight lines. The right back and the right midfielder, the central defenders and central midfielders and the left back and left midfielder all just worked up and down the pitch in straight lines which they rarely deviated from (figure 23). But here were such talented players, all so in tune with each other, that they were able to interchange all over the pitch without ever losing the team's shape or balance (figure 24).

Of the four midfield players, Nobby Stiles had a purely defensive job to do. Nobby was not in the team to spray balls about; he broke play up, he tackled people, he won things. Bobby Charlton would usually be found ahead of Stiles in central areas, running with the ball, shooting from distance, or playing forty- or fifty-yard balls. In the 1966 World Cup Final Ramsey detailed him to shadow the great German midfielder Franz Beckenbauer. Little did he know that Beckenbauer had been told to shadow Charlton and as a consequence both players had less of an influence on this particular game than they would normally have had.

Martin Peters, who lined up on the left but had licence to roam, was the kind of player who arrived in the penalty area late. If the play was on the left he would drift away to the right and if people were caught ball watching he would sneak in at the back. Alan Ball was a revelation. He was brilliant all over the pitch. He ran and ran and ran. His job was to get the ball and influence the play. When England had the ball he would support Hunt and Hurst up front, usually on the right, and when they didn't have it, he would drop back into midfield to defend. When England were attacking they played a 4–3–3 formation, with Alan Ball the more likely midfielder to push into attack. But when they were defending it would be 4–4–2, with Ball dropping into the midfield to help out (figures 25a and b). This was only possible because of the phenomenal amount of ground that Ball could cover.

There must have been many England fans who wondered how England would get a cross into the box without a winger. But good

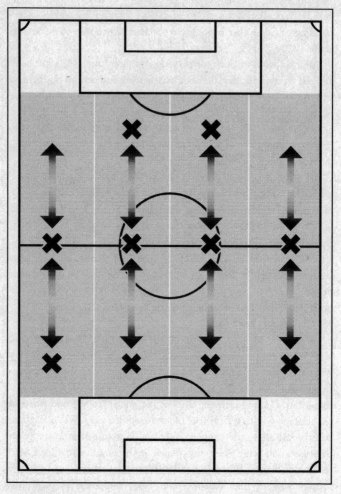

Figure 23: Rigid 4–4–2, where players are restricted to playing up and down the pitch in straight lines. Solid but uninspiring

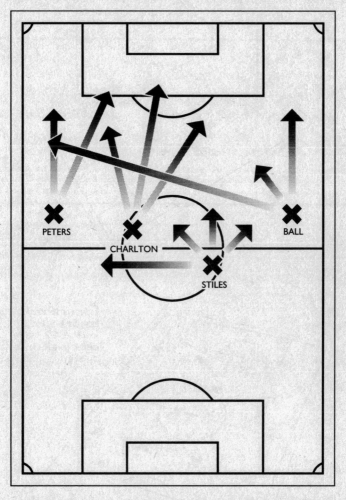

Figure 24: The 1966 England team played four in midfield, but it was a constantly switching, fluid four

Figure 25(a)

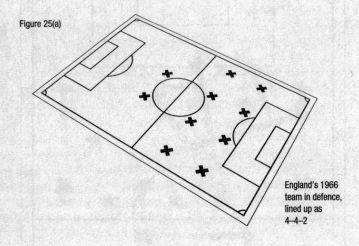

England's 1966 team in defence, lined up as 4–4–2

(b)

England on the attack, more like 4–3–3 or sometimes 4–2–4 as the midfield goes on the offensive

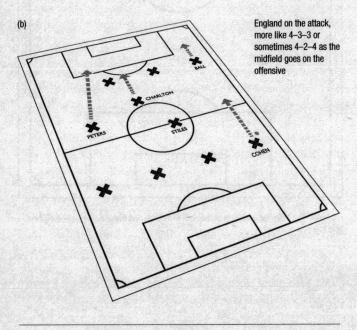

players have a knack of working the ball into areas from where the ball can be crossed. The full backs were vitally important in this respect, George Cohen and Ray Wilson getting forward as often as possible to provide width. But they didn't take big risks for fear of leaving themselves open to the counter attack. They were happy to fire crosses in from deep – not from the area ten to fifteen yards from the by-line on the edge of the box where a winger would but from thirty or forty yards from the line – and rely on Hurst's and Hunt's ability in the air to make something happen.

An interesting thing about the 1966 final is that the feeling before-hand was that the German goalkeeper, Tilkowski, was very weak on crosses (the joke doing the rounds at the World Cup was that his nick-name was 'Dracula' because he was so afraid of them) and many people believed that Ramsey would revert to playing wingers specifi-cally for this game to get crosses in and put him under pressure. But such was the quality of the players that he had, the two full backs and the people getting wide, that he decided to stick with the plan that had got him to the final. They knew they were going to get crosses in anyway and they didn't want to sacrifice what they had, namely a rock-solid midfield.

Up front Geoff Hurst of West Ham and Roger Hunt of Liverpool were just left to play. There was nothing particularly unusual about this pairing, although they were about the hardest working striking partnership you will ever see. I think that's probably why Ramsey couldn't find a place in the team for Jimmy Greaves when he recov-ered from his injury. He was the most talented striker in the country at the time – at the start of the tournament he was England's all-time leading scorer with forty-three goals – but Ramsey needed more than a goalscorer. He needed his wide men to have defensive duties and the same applied to his strikers. I think he thought he needed players who were going to work hard and defend from the front for the entire ninety minutes. Greavsie was a prolific, natural goalscorer but Ramsey wanted his strikers to work their bodies into their ground and that simply wasn't the way Greaves played.

With Hunt and Hurst you had two players who were great in the air, and they thrived on crosses coming in from anywhere in the area alongside the eighteen-yard box – the classic area for a winger. However, England weren't able to get the ball in those areas an awful lot. That was the only thing that was lacking with this system. But I think they were happy to fire it in from further out, Cohen and Wilson crossing it in from thirty yards out, and maybe even further.

The full backs would advance only so far. Normally – when they were playing in a 4–2–4 – there would have been someone wide for them to pass to, namely the winger. But since they had no one to give the ball to who would take it a stage further, the full backs had to fire the ball into the box from deep. They could have tried to take on a player or two to to get into a position closer to goal, but if they did this and were tackled and lost the ball they would be leaving a dangerous gap behind them which could be exploited by a quick counter-attack. So Cohen and Wilson angled balls in from deep. If you look at the game the first time England get the ball to the by-line is well into the second half and it's Roger Hunt of all people who finds himself there to put in a cross.

The game was so open in 1966. Teams hardly ever played offside. You never saw back fours push with their arms in the air. They defended properly, and the game was played from box to box with hardly any offsides at all. For Germany's first goal, Siggy Held's cross was headed out and as Helmut Haller knocked it in to score Jack Charlton was standing two yards away from his own goal line. You just wouldn't see that nowadays. He would have pushed out to the edge of the penalty area. But the game was so much simpler then. When you had the ball you charged forward, when you lost it you charged back. By having four midfielders coming back to defend Ramsey built a team which was harder to open up and harder to score against but was still fast, skilful and creative going forward.

Another important factor in Ramsey's team was the West Ham connection. Moore, Peters and Hurst had all played together for years in a West Ham side which won the FA Cup in 1964 and the European Cup Winners' Cup the following year with both finals, incidentally, being played at Wembley. So there was a connection from back to front of players who knew how each other played. In a system where there was so much flexibility, so much interchanging of positions, that was important. Just look at England's first goal. While everyone else has gone to sleep Bobby Moore steps into the midfield to launch a quick free kick into the box where he finds his West Ham colleague Geoff Hurst all on his own. He bangs it in with his head and England are back in the game.

After that goal England really controlled the match. They had most of the pressure and most of the chances and deservedly won, even if it took extra time and the incredible eyesight of a Russian linesman to do it.

The 1966 World Cup Final was highly influential in the evolution of the British game. A lot of English club sides started playing the way Ramsey had sent out his team. Of course, many sides had great wingers in their squads so they didn't change their style immediately, but everyone was aware of the differing role of the wide player in top level football.

A player like Alan Ball epitomised the change. The result told the Football League that wingers still had a place but that the Alan Balls of this world – players who could provide width but could also come inside as well as drop back and help in defence – could be more useful. With this new wide player it was as though you had two players where before you had only one, a pure, touchline-hugging out-and-out attacker. Coaches started looking for that type of player. They were looking for versatility and the end product was super-versatile wide men like Steve Coppell who played 320 league games for Manchester United between 1974 and 1982 and Trevor Steven, who was a major reason why the Everton side I played in during the 1980s was such a force.

Even before Ramsey's team traditional wingers were always regarded as lazy as hell. They stood on the touchline waiting until they got the ball, then tried to beat three players and cross it into the box. The new players were so different. They became the hardest working players on the pitch because they had two jobs. It's a role that men like Ryan Giggs perform right now. Although everyone thinks of Giggs terrorising defences by running at them at speed, you just watch the work he puts in helping out his defence when United haven't got possession. On the other hand, take, for example, David

Ginola when he was at Newcastle, a more traditional, out-and-out winger. What a player, what ability. But how many managers in the Premiership can afford the luxury of having a man in the team who, when he loses the ball, just stands up front waiting until he gets it back? These players should be tigerishly helping their full backs when their team hasn't got the ball. Then, within seconds, they should be steaming up the other end of the pitch, influencing the play in the attacking third and helping the forwards. To his credit, Ginola has done that at Spurs with a move into a more central midfield area.

The best players in the world, and I defy anyone to tell me otherwise, will always be the hardest working ones. Pele, Johan Cruyff and Maradona worked incredibly hard. They didn't just rely on skill and ability. The best teams are always full of great players with great skill and great ability, but they don't carry anyone. They all work their guts off. You can go through history and look at incredibly talented players who never made it at the top level – Matt Le Tissier, Tony Currie – and the one thing that they haven't had is work rate. It's a horrible word and some might argue that you don't need it, but, believe me, you do. The 1966 England team had it in abundance.

People ask me if I think the 1966 World Cup-winning side could have survived in the modern game and my answer is always 'yes'. But they would have to push up at the back – they couldn't allow other teams as much time and space as they allowed them then. They could survive, firstly because when they lost the ball they could make themselves difficult to play against. They worked hard from front to back. But then, more importantly, when they had the ball they had the freedom and the quality to pass the ball about, influence the game and hurt teams at the other end of the pitch.

If you were to ask me if 2–3–5 could survive in the modern game then I would probably say 'no'. Apart from that you can play any system you want in football if you have great players. But in 1966 someone still had to put the right players into the right system. Someone still had to have the vision and the conviction to find the right players and make them into a team, a team playing to a revolutionary plan and a system. Alf Ramsey chose the players and the formation for the 1966 World Cup and he got it right. It just proves that you can take a bunch of players and, with hours of graft on the training pitch, coach them into playing a completely new system. But, like any system, you can coach it a hell of a lot easier when you're doing it with world-class players.

CHAPTER 5
4–4–2 and 4–2–4

4–4–2 is the system you are most likely to see when you turn up at any ground in Britain at 3 pm on a Saturday afternoon. Take a look at Manchester United. Week in week out it's 4–4–2. Take a look at Arsenal, take a look at Blackburn, take a look even at Chelsea. After a first season where former boss Ruud Gullit played five at the back religiously, as his predecessor Glenn Hoddle had done, even the most flamboyant foreign coach in the English game started the 1997/98 campaign playing 4–4–2.

Four at the back gives you a solid base as a platform for attack. Having four in midfield in front of that four in defence gives you protection. It's not cavalier. But it ensures that you build from a position of strength. When your side doesn't have the ball it means that effectively you have eight men back (figure 26).

When you do get the ball 4–4–2 gives you lots of little pockets where you have two or three players close to each other who can start working little triangles together. When Gary Neville wins the ball at right back for Manchester United you can almost visualise his options. He will have the option of a little ball back into his centre back (Ronny Johnsen or Gary Pallister). Just ahead of him will be David Beckham but he can also play a short diagonal ball in to Nicky Butt. These players can work the ball between them, advancing the play and bringing Sheringham or Scholes into the play or switching to the other side when the moment is right (figure 27).

With 4–4–2 players are never isolated, either with or without the ball. It's all about working little triangles of players who work

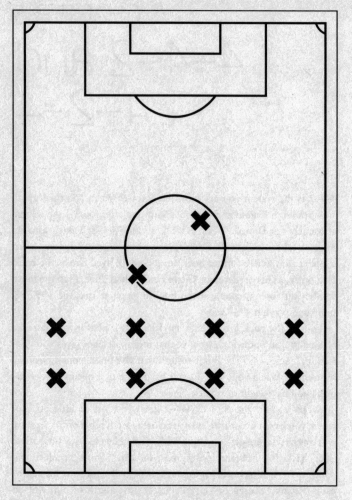

Figure 26: 4–4–2 in defence, with two banks of four players providing blanket cover

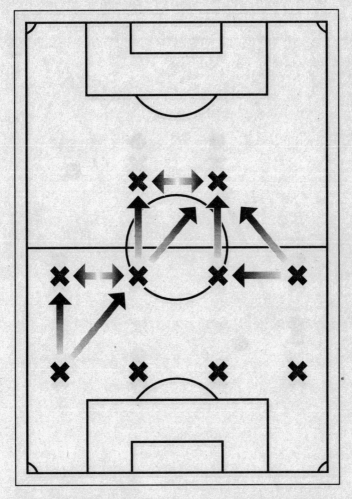

Figure 27: With 4–4–2 you have several pockets of three or four players close together who can play in little triangles

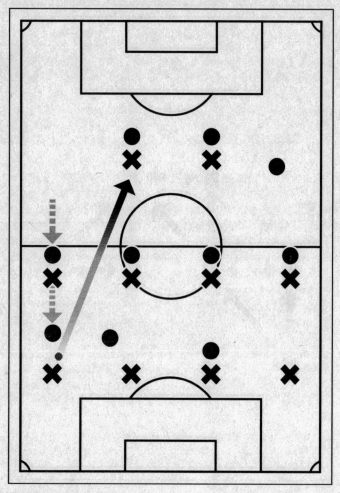

Figure 28: The out ball

together trying to get the ball up the pitch, with the front two providing the out-ball if needed (figure 28). Then as soon as the ball is lost again the four in defence and the four in midfield drop back to provide a blanket of cover.

When people talk about defending they usually think only about the back four or the back five, but all eleven players on the pitch are the defence when your team hasn't got the ball. No team could ever get away with having just four great defenders. That's the beauty of playing 4–4–2. It means the defence and midfield double up whenever the team has to defend. You always have teams of two all over the pitch. The right back and the right midfielder work together. The centre backs and the central midfielders work together and the left back and the left midfielder work together. Two banks of four protect your goal.

The current Manchester United side is possibly the best example I've ever seen of a back four that's so well protected it's hard to see a way to score against them. At home Fergie sometimes likes to play with three strikers in a 4–3–3 system but generally it's 4–4–2. In this system the two central midfield players, say Keane and Butt, do the most magnificent job of protecting their back four. In wide areas Ryan Giggs and David Beckham are famous for their marauding forward play, but, believe you me, they're in there battling as if their lives depended on it whenever the opposition is going forward.

But it goes back even further than that. Your first line of defence is your front two, there's no doubt about that. They work across the pitch trying to make sure the opposition defenders don't have time on the ball to pick out a pass.

I think the team that runs Manchester United pretty close as great exponents of classic 4–4–2 is Blackburn. The team which won the Premier League in 1995 were as good an example of 4–4–2 as you could ever hope to see. And with Roy Hodgson they've got back to a similar standard. My vision of 4–4–2 is how Blackburn play, with Ripley and Wilcox working overtime on the flanks, wingers one minute and full backs the next. They have two great central defenders in Hendry and Henchoz and the two front men, Sutton and Gallacher, are not only a threat but work their socks off when the opposition has the ball.

Brian Clough was a 4–4–2 man to the core. His teams always had two banks of four. It was the system he played when he won the title with Nottingham Forest in 1978 and when he won the European Cup in 1979 and 1980. The Everton side I was part of in the mid-1980s was the best side in which I ever played and we used this system. When we stood in the tunnel waiting to run out onto the pitch at Goodison Park we just knew we were going to win. We were that confident in our system.

At Everton in those days we had the perfect back four to play 4–4–2. It was a back four that was as quick as I have ever seen, and if you have that then you're in heaven. The whole unit was less likely to get caught out by a nippy striker or a ball over the top and more likely to be able to recover if it was caught out. It could also contribute in attacking areas.

We had two great centre backs in Kevin Ratcliffe and Derek Mountfield. They were big, strong men who would fight for, and more often than not win, everything. We had Gary Stevens at right back and Pat Van Den Hauwe at left back, both incredibly fit lads with great powers of recovery. Van Den Hauwe was probably a slightly better user of the ball but Gary Stevens had an unbelievable engine. He could get forward at will but was always back in there when needed. As soon as the ball went left he would jog back into position to help out his centre backs and if it went right he would belt forward and Pat would tuck back in.

Then we had two tigers in central midfield in Peter Reid and Paul Bracewell, who not only protected the back four but also, when they got the ball, had the ability to pass it and bring other players into the game. These positions are crucial in a 4–4–2 formation. It's so important that they work hard to defend and protect the back four, but if they can use the ball like Peter and Paul did for us, or how Ince and Redknapp do at Liverpool, then you've got everything you could possibly ask for from your central midfielders.

Then we had two wide men in Kevin Sheedy and Trevor Steven who were fantastic on the ball. They had a great range of passing and both could score goals. They had to work so hard up and down the pitch it was untrue, but that relentless movement up and down the wing is crucial to the success of 4–4–2. Trevor knew that if Kevin was crossing a ball in from the left he had to get into the box along with the strikers – myself and Graeme Sharp – and probably one of the central midfielders as well, but if we lost the ball he had to charge back and provide cover for Pat at left back.

Compared to him I suppose Graeme and I had an easy life as the two up front. But we still worked incredibly hard defensively as well as in attack, closing down the space when our opponents' back four had the ball and generally making a nuisance of ourselves.

We had the perfect balance for a team playing classic 4–4–2 and I honestly can't think of anybody who I could have put in there that would have made us any better, and that's saying something.

Eric Cantona talked about 4–4–2 when I did *The Boot Room* with him for Sky Sports in 1995. He was talking about AC Milan, saying it was his favourite team, and that if he was a manager he would play their system. It was noticeable that, during the mid-1980s, Arrigo Sacchi, Milan's manager, decided that what he had seen in England was good enough to put into practice in *Serie A*. Sacchi abandoned the sweeper system traditionally favoured by Italian sides and played a back four which pushed up the field, looking to play their opponents offside. On top of that they had four in midfield and two up front, and they dominated Italy and Europe with this system. Milan had a back four which played in the normal way with the great Franco Baresi as the governor, dictating when they pushed up. But the subtle difference with the Milan side was in the midfield. When the four in midfield won the ball they would line up in the usual way, in a line of four across the pitch. But when they lost it, the four would hunt in a pack. They would all charge in towards the ball, working in a tight square, pressing the opposition and hunting the ball (figures 29a, b and c). This became known as the pressing game.

I asked Eric what would happen if the opposition just changed the play, switching the ball to the other side? Surely, I argued, the entire midfield would then be caught on the wrong side of the pitch, leaving acres of room to attack. But he said that this wouldn't be a problem because the four midfielders were so quick and mobile that it wouldn't take them long to get back across to the ball. The opposition, he

Figure 29(a)

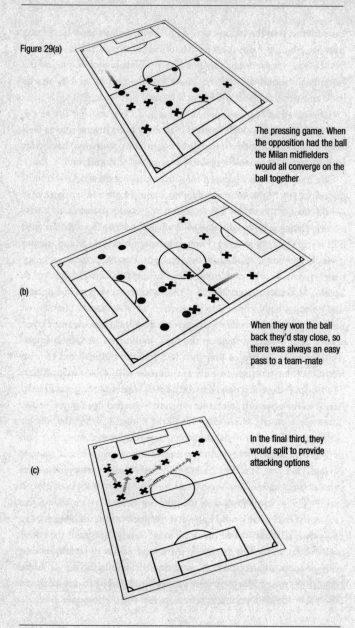

The pressing game. When the opposition had the ball the Milan midfielders would all converge on the ball together

(b)

When they won the ball back they'd stay close, so there was always an easy pass to a team-mate

(c)

In the final third, they would split to provide attacking options reasoned, would only have time to cross the ball in from deep before the four players were upon them, and Milan's defenders were so good that they would be confident of dealing with this sort of ball anyway. As the four midfielders were so quick and so abrasive, the situation rarely arose because more often than not they won the ball before it could be switched.

I remember Cantona saying to me that Manchester United could not win the European Cup if they played with two wide midfielders who never came infield. At the time they were playing with Giggs on the left and Kanchelskis on the right, almost as old style out-and-out wingers, but Eric wanted Alex Ferguson to play the Milan system. To an extent I think Fergie has done that now. The midfield has become much, much more compact. Giggs still gets wide but he's become much more of a complete player. He tracks back, he cuts inside and, crucially, he presses, harries and tackles when the other side is in possession. It's the same with Beckham when he's playing on the right. So Ferguson hasn't gone all the way down the route of Milan's pressing game, but he has gone halfway there from where he was, and he's started to experience far greater success on the European stage.

Of course, to make it work, Sacchi's team had to work like mad. That's the thing about systems and tactics, they only work if the players believe in them and the players make them work. If you looked at that midfield you saw four lads working their bodies into the ground.

The diamond formation is another variation of traditional 4–4–2. Instead of playing in a straight line across the pitch the four midfield players play roughly in the shape of – yes, you guessed it – a diamond. A holding player sits just in front of the centre backs and provides defensive cover. Then you have two who play just ahead of him – one on the right and one on the left – who are creative players. They will go wide when necessary but will also play through the middle, and when the other team has the ball they must tuck in and work to get it back. Then ahead of them, at the top of the diamond, is a more attacking player. This would be someone like Teddy Sheringham or Juninho, playing in 'the hole' (see Chapter Eight), sitting in behind the front two, a player who wouldn't be expected to get back and defend nearly as much as his colleagues in the diamond.

This system works well when you don't have good wide players such as Blackburn have in Wilcox and Ripley but you have midfield players like Beckham who can go wide but would prefer to play infield. Then having someone like Darren Anderton on the other side would be ideal. At the base of the diamond the ideal player would be someone like David Batty who's great at breaking up the play, getting the ball and just laying it off neatly. At the top you need someone like Paul Scholes, a good attacking player but one with the vision and craft to create chances for the more traditional front men with little flicks and passes threaded through the defence. Beckham, Anderton, Batty and Scholes would make a pretty compact yet creative diamond midfield.

During the 1970s a version of 4–4–2 was developed in Holland which was to take world football by storm. 'Total football', as it was known, was a system which relied on the complete versatility of the players who played it. First developed at Ajax under manager Rinus Michels, the system was 4–4–2 on paper but the players constantly switched positions. The play had a liquid, fluent quality. The great Johan Cruyff was the conductor of the Ajax orchestra. Nominally a centre forward, in reality Cruyff played all over the pitch, dragging defenders with him so that midfielders and full backs could exploit the gaps they left. If the centre backs went forward with the ball, midfielders would drop into their place. If Cruyff came into defence to pick it up one of the centre backs would push forward. Every player in the team was a master of the ball – men like Neeskens, Krol and Rep – and Ajax won the European Cup three years in a row in 1971, 1972 and 1973.

When they didn't have the ball they hunted it ravenously, when they did have it they moved and switched with such speed and style that defences were often ripped apart. The 'total football' philosophy is still very much at the heart of the modern Ajax and at their famous school of excellence, young players play in every position on the pitch – including goalkeeper – until the age of fourteen, to make them aware of the intricacies of every role in a football team.

'Total football' was a redefinition of the individual player's role. Where once he was strictly an attacker, a midfielder or a defender, in this system every player became an interchangeable part of a machine that was constantly in motion. In 1973 Cruyff and Neeskens moved to Barcelona but Michels took charge of the Dutch national team and, playing the same way, Holland reached the World Cup Finals of 1974 and 1978, unluckily losing both.

Yet another adaptation of classic 4–4–2 is when teams play more of a 4–2–4 formation. Teams that use this system line up in the traditional 4–4–2. The difference is that when they get the ball the two wide midfield players push right forward alongside their two strikers (figure 30). It's a question of really taking a chance in throwing four up against four.

These days you tend to see 4–2–4 being played when teams are playing a direct game, trying to get the ball forward quickly. Wimbledon do it brilliantly. We all know that Wimbledon don't really like to pass the ball about in midfield, so when they gain possession there's no real point in having the two wide midfielders sitting in alongside Vinnie Jones and Robbie Earle in the centre of midfield. They're not going to get the ball there. So Joe Kinnear puts them right up alongside the strikers so that when it comes from one of the full backs or from the goalkeeper these players are suddenly in the game.

In the modern game you will rarely see a team playing a traditional 4–2–4 system – basically a way of accommodating two wingers. This was once some teams' only real form of attack but these days you will never see a team with four strikers standing in a line with their hands on their hips waiting for the ball to come back to them. The system Wimbledon play is effectively two systems. It's one system when they don't have the ball and another when they do.

When Kevin Keegan was manager of Newcastle United his team played a kind of 4–4–2, but I'm not sure that there are words to describe his system. The problem was that Keegan's system wasn't built on solid foundations. For 4–4–2 to work the back four must work. What was ahead of the back four in Kevin's side was fantastic. He had the likes of Ferdinand, Asprilla and Shearer providing an awesome strikeforce and Robert Lee, David Ginola and Keith Gillespie in a highly skilful and attacking midfield, but the back four – of say Beresford, Peacock, Albert and Barton – simply wasn't solid enough.

They virtually played a back five system, but they were a man

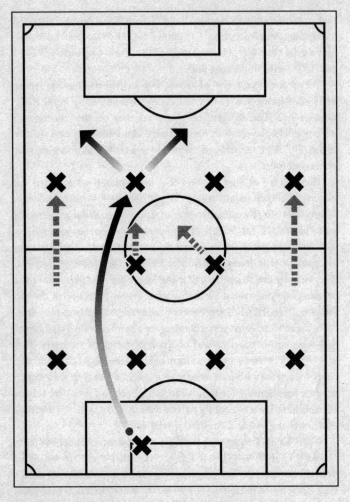

Figure 30: 4–2–4 in the modern game, where wide midfielders push into attack in anticipation of a long ball up front

short. When they had the ball both full backs would go flying forward like wing backs, leaving two defenders to mark two strikers (figure 31). This was suicidal, because when you are defending you should always have a spare man as cover. So when Newcastle lost the ball and the other team knocked it back into their half, neither full back was there to provide cover and the poor centre backs had to try and deal with the danger on their own.

It would be a bit harsh to blame the full backs because Kevin Keegan must have told them to push forward at every opportunity. It must have been a specific tactic. I can't believe that Keegan, having been at Liverpool all those years, wouldn't have coached his players into making sure that there was always one full back in place to cover for the centre backs.

At some stage Kevin must have sat down and thought that by playing this way he could win games, presumably banking on the philosophy that if the opposition scored three goals his team would score four. To be fair, a lot of the time it worked for him, although it was just as likely that Newcastle would score three times and the other team would get four. It provided us all with a great deal of entertainment, but it was a system that was never going to win him a title. History shows us that invariably the best defence in the land wins the league, not the highest scorers.

As soon as Kenny Dalglish took over at St James' Park we immediately saw a totally new and different Newcastle. I watched them play Sheffield Wednesday on the opening day of the 1997/98 season at home. They were 2–1 up late in the game and I was thinking that if I had been watching Kevin's side they would have been looking for a third and a fourth, leaving themselves vulnerable at the back and maybe conceding one to make it 2–2. Dalglish's side, on the other hand, controlled the game and protected their 2–1 lead. That's the difference.

So maybe 4–4–2 isn't exciting. Maybe it's not exotic or 'sexy' as Ruud Gullit might say. But it's the system that gives you the best balance between defence and attack, and I would send my team out playing it every day of the week whether they were playing Brazil or Bromsgrove Wanderers.

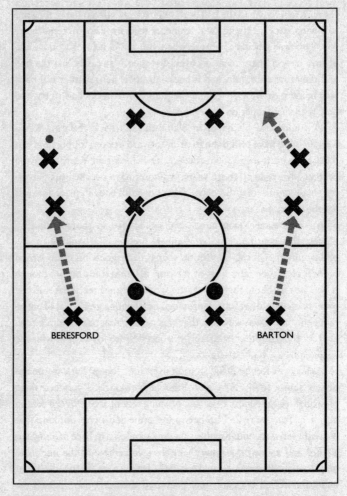

Figure 31: Newcastle's 'suicidal' system. Both full backs, Beresford and Barton, would push forward at the same time leaving two against two at the back

CHAPTER 6
Celtic 1967

● ●

CELTIC 2 INTER MILAN 1
25 May 1967 (European Cup Final)
National Stadium, Lisbon. Attendance: 55,000.

Celtic: (4–2–4)

Simpson

Gemmell	Clark	McNeill	Craig
	Auld	Murdoch	
Jonhstone	Chalmers	Wallace	Lennox

Inter Milan: Sarti, Burgnich, Guarneri, Facchetti, Bedin, Picchi, Domenghini, Mazzola, Cappellini, Bicicli, Corso

Roared on by 12,000 travelling Scots, Celtic's bid to become the first British side to win the European Cup started badly. The one thing you didn't want to do against Inter Milan was concede an early goal, so when the Italians were awarded a penalty in the eighth minute for a foul by full back Jim Craig the writing, it seemed, was on the wall. Mazzola converted the kick and it was 1–0 to Inter. But Celtic came back. Their famous green and white shirts swarmed around the Inter box, but chance after chance went begging. In the second half Bertie Auld hit the bar then Tommy Gemmell rattled the woodwork. It was agonising to watch. Then, in the sixty-third minute, Craig centred to

*his fellow full back Gemmell on the edge of the box, and he unleashed
the shot of his life. The ball flew into the top corner and Celtic were
level. The Celtic fans – many of them waving huge, green shamrocks
– went mad, but that was nothing compared to the scenes seven
minutes from time when, with Celtic now attacking like their lives
depended on it, Bobby Murdoch's shot cannoned off Steve Chalmers
into the back of the net. It was 2–1 to Celtic and there was to be no
way back for Inter.*

The 1967 European Cup Final was just about the biggest clash of
footballing styles you could ever imagine. It was a meeting of two
teams who inhabited opposite ends of the tactical spectrum. Jock
Stein's Celtic played in the traditional Scottish way with two out-and-
out wingers and a basic philosophy of all-out attack while Helenio
Herrera's Inter Milan, the pioneers of *catenaccio* (the door bolt)
defending, with four man markers and a sweeper, excelled at grinding
out 1–0 wins.

For many this game was more than a battle for the European Cup,
it was a kind of good v evil contest with Celtic on some kind of
crusade to save free-flowing attacking football from extinction. As a
Rangers fan I didn't quite see it that way, of course, and it hurt like
hell to see the arch enemy become the first British team to lift that
famous trophy. But, in truth, Celtic were magnificent that day.

While many teams in England had been influenced by Alf
Ramsey's 'wingless wonders', most Scottish teams had retained the
4–2–4 approach and Celtic were by far the most effective at its execution. With skilful wingers Jimmy Johnstone and Bobby Lennox at the
heart of everything they did, 1966/67 was the season in which they
were truly unstoppable. They won the European Cup, the Scottish
League, the Scottish Cup and the Scottish League Cup. Yet before the
European Cup Final most people still believed that Inter Milan would
simply be too strong for them.

Inter's so-called *catenaccio* defensive system was feared and
revered all over the footballing world. It had evolved from the first
sweeper system, the brainchild of Austrian coach Karl Rappan, who
introduced it when coach of the Swiss national team in the 1937/38

season. Concerned that whenever the opposition's centre forward managed to get past his centre half he was clean through on goal, Rappan withdrew one of the three strikers from the head of his 'WM' formation and replaced him with an extra defender positioned in front of the goalkeeper.

Rappan christened his system the *verrou* or 'door bolt' system and his extra defender the *verrouller*, and Swiss fortunes improved immediately. They beat England 2–1 in a friendly in May 1938 and a few weeks later knocked Germany out of the World Cup. Unlike later sweepers like Franz Beckenbauer or the Dutchman Ronald Koeman, Rappan's *verrouller* was entirely defensive, and it was this added security at the back which inspired Argentinian coach Helenio Herrera to develop a similar system when he became coach at Inter in the 1960s.

Herrera's system involved four defenders who were tight man-to-man markers. This meant that each defender was assigned to mark a particular attacker – and stuck to him like glue wherever he went to try and ensure he never had the space to pose a threat on goal. Playing behind these four man-markers for Inter was the sweeper. The idea was that he would pick up anything that came through the back four. Popping up here, there and everywhere he would sweep up wherever and whenever he was needed. He was Inter's safety valve (figure 32).

Herrera detailed Armando Picchi to play this role for Inter in what was effectively a 1–4–3–1 formation (figure 33), with five defenders who really did do nothing but defend. The strategy was to try to nick an early goal on the counter-attack and then shut up shop with the three midfielders sitting in front of the back four. It was a case of score a goal, bring down the shutters and wait for the final whistle. And it worked.

In 1964 Inter beat Real Madrid 3–1 (an unusually high-scoring performance) to win the European Cup and they retained the trophy the following year, defeating Benfica of Portugal with a more characteristic 1–0 victory. In a period of four years Inter reached the final of the competition three times (1964, 1965 and 1967 – they narrowly lost in the semi-finals to the eventual winners, Real Madrid, in 1966). Virtually impossible to score against, prior to reaching the 1967 final against Celtic their scores in their nine previous matches

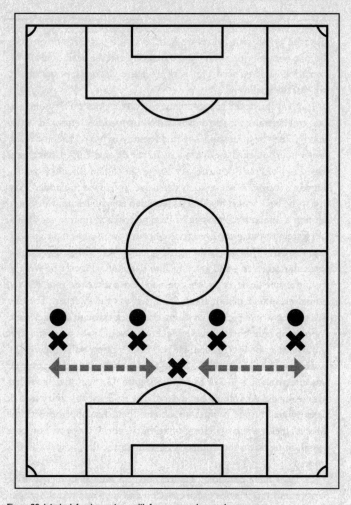

Figure 32: Inter's defensive system, with four man markers and a sweeper

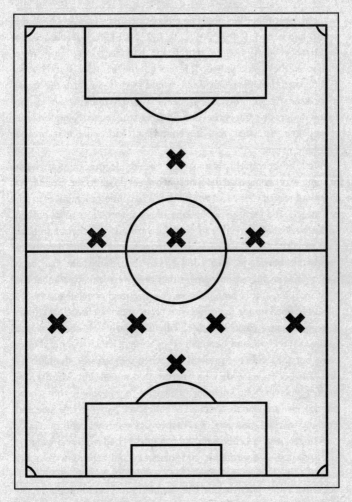

Figure 33: Inter's 1–4–3–1 formation

in the competition (they needed a replay to get past CSKA Sofia in the semis) had been 1–0, 0–0, 2–1, 2–0, 1–0, 2–0, 1–1, 1–1 and 1–0.

Of those that thought that Celtic had a chance, most were convinced they could only do it if they got the first goal. If Inter went 1–0 up then that, people believed, would be that. So when the nightmare scenario unfolded, most people started thinking about the following year's competition and Rangers fans started uncorking the champagne. So what was it about that Celtic side that proved everyone wrong?

Well, in short, Celtic were such a formidable attacking force that in some ways going a goal down suited them down to the ground. As Inter had scored Celtic had no choice but to commit themselves to all-out attack, and because the Italians allowed themselves to be pushed so far back they were able to pour forward and pin them into their own penalty area. Most teams would have found the Inter defence an impossible barrier to break down even then, but Celtic had such quality and such great movement that they were able to combat the tight marking and fashion chances. It was a mighty achievement.

Celtic lined up for the game with pretty much a classic back four. They had centre backs Billy McNeill and John Clark and two good full backs in Craig and Gemmell. They were defenders first and foremost but they didn't get nosebleeds when they crossed the halfway line. Further forward they had Bertie Auld and Bobby Murdoch in midfield, players who knew their defensive responsibilities but whose natural instinct was to attack. The difference between this side and England in 1966, however, was that to Celtic this was still the era of the winger. And in Lennox and Johnstone they had two great wingers.

It was a 4–2–4 formation and Johnstone and Lennox were in the side to contribute to the attack. But I wouldn't say these two had no defensive duties whatsoever. They wouldn't just stand on the touchline waiting for the ball in the way that Stanley Matthews did in the 1940s and 1950s. You didn't win all the games that Celtic did in those days with two players not getting back and helping out at all. However, it was not their priority. When they lost the ball you would never see them sprinting fifty yards to get back into defence and then sprinting fifty yards to get back up again as Ryan Giggs does these days for Manchester United.

I played against Johnstone and Lennox when I was at Dundee United and they were fabulous players. Johnstone was somebody who you could give a ball to on a football pitch and he would still have it five minutes later. He would have beaten twenty-five men and he wouldn't have moved ten yards from the spot where he received the ball. He was aptly nicknamed 'Jinky' and his ability to twist and turn was something the like of which I hadn't seen before and I haven't seen since. The only modern-day footballer that even resembles him, but certainly doesn't compete, is Pat Nevin, who used to play for Chelsea, Everton and Scotland. On the other side you had the pace and directness of Bobby Lennox. Bobby was tremendously quick and he used his pace to get past people. He would just fizz the ball past players and run after it.

These two players were Celtic's creators, but they couldn't do it on their own. After Inter scored their penalty in the eighth minute, the Scots were faced with a barricade between them and the goal, the like of which they would never have seen before. They were playing against a side which simply didn't give goals away, a side which always had enough spare men at the back and a side which always marked tightly.

If you look at a modern back four, when the opposition has the ball they mark their men closely but not too close. It's too risky. It means if they are beaten by a sharp turn or quick piece of skill their opponent is away from them. They will let an attacking player have the ball, drop off a yard and challenge him to get past. But the Inter defenders could stick right on the Celtic attackers, getting as tight as they liked, because they knew that they had the safety of the sweeper behind them.

After they had gone one down Celtic had to commit the whole team – with the exception of the two centre backs – to attack. But this was not such a bad thing, because attacking was what they did best anyway. The two midfield players, Bobby Murdoch and Bertie Auld, were very positive-thinking players and because Inter weren't coming forward at all they simply joined the attack. And when Johnstone and Lennox drifted infield from the wide areas, their markers went with them, leaving an incredible amount of space for the full backs, Tommy Gemmell and Jim Craig, to attack.

For much of the game both Celtic full backs surged forward at the same time. I remember Jim Craig telling me that when he played right back for his school team his teacher had told him that he should never cross the halfway line – that was pretty much the thinking in those days – and suddenly here he was playing as a right winger. Celtic could only do this, leaving just their two centre backs defending, because the Italians were only playing with one up front.

Because of the way the Italians played, this tactic wasn't as risky as, say, when full backs Beresford and Barton used to charge forward at the same time for Newcastle under Kevin Keegan, because their opponents were generally playing with two up front. Celtic wouldn't ever have taken such a risk in a Scottish League game, because the good teams would have caught them out. You can imagine Tommy Gemmell and Jim Craig playing against a team which played the same way as Celtic in Scotland. Their opponents would normally have played with four up front and they would have stayed back and marked the opposition wingers. That was their job. But on this occasion, Gemmell and Craig didn't have anybody to mark, and suddenly they had all this space ahead of them. Full marks to them, then, for being good enough and brave enough to go forward into the space and use it to good effect.

When Celtic went into all-out attack, it must have been a huge shock to Inter. Their gameplan was to defend in numbers, but also to try and get hold of the ball and pass it around to take the sting out of the game. But Celtic threw so many men forward, men playing with fantastic movement and flair, that Inter were pinned right back onto the edge of their area for virtually the entire eighty-two minutes of the game that were left after they scored. They were squeezed back into the danger area by seven or eight Celtic players swarming all over them, something that would never have happened in the Italian League. No other team would have attacked in this way. Inter weren't allowed to pass the ball about, and because they were pegged so far back there was no room behind the defence for Picchi to sweep up in his usual manner.

Like all Scottish clubs at the time, Celtic would try to win the ball as high up the pitch as possible. Whereas in Italy the Inter sweeper would get time to pick the ball up from the goalie, play a few passes and link with the midfield, Celtic didn't give him that chance. When the ball was in the Inter keeper's hands, or when it was a goal kick, Celtic pushed up from the back and cut out that route. After Inter scored they never got the chance to knock the ball around and kill the play, so their defence was always under pressure. Inter were not allowed to get the ball down and pass it across the back and into midfield, which would normally have been their break from defending.

When Inter went 1–0 up they thought they had won the game. But they hadn't accounted for the spirit and belief of Celtic. Jock Stein was the master of man management and he seemed to be able to get the best out of any player he ever coached. Before the match Inter stayed in a military-style training camp with the doors locked and the press kept well away. Jock, on the other hand, booked his team into a hotel where the door was always open and it was like a big party. The press were there, the players' families were there, and they were so laid back they were almost horizontal.

They had a great laugh with Jock. Apparently, a day or so before the game, they had a training session in the stadium. Naturally Inter had sent their spies to observe, so Jock organised a practice match for their benefit. A strange tactic, you might think, except that he played everyone out of position. He put the centre backs on the wings and the wingers in defence, the front men in midfield and the full backs up front. I would have loved to have heard the report Herrera's scouts sent back.

Before the game the Celtic players sang the 'Celtic Song' in the tunnel to the bemusement of the Inter players. Stein then purposely went and sat in the seat on the touchline which Herrera had earmarked for himself and refused to budge. Herrera was said to be absolutely furious by this, but the Celtic players thought it was hilarious.

A consequence of Jock's man management was that Celtic had the self-belief, the confidence and the spirit to recover from being 1–0 down to this formidable defensive team. And when Inter invited them to come forward it gave them time and space to gain confidence on the ball. So Celtic grew and grew in stature and eventually Inter's ultra-defensive tactics backfired.

Celtic combated the Inter system by flying forward with the type of skilful, incisive attacks which you can only mount if you have players on board like Jimmy Johnstone. To break down a system like Inter's you either need players who can take the ball when tightly marked but still turn defenders or you need players with good movement who can take defenders into places they don't want to go. Celtic had both.

Apart from his defence, Jock Stein had no restrictions for his players. He never restricted Lennox, Wallace, Chalmers and Johnstone and I think that Inter underestimated them. When Inter scored it freed Celtic. They just knew they had to go for it. They had to score to have any chance in the game, and they knew that to score they would have to attack in droves. From the moment they kicked off after conceding that early goal Celtic created chance after chance.

What always amazed me about *catenaccio* was that the Italian teams which played the system had such good players, but as soon as they went 1–0 up they went right back into their shells. After they scored in the eighth minute Inter went 1–4–4–1, effectively with nine men defending. In their defence, they were missing their main playmaker, the Spaniard Suarez, but I'm sure they would still have played the same way.

The spirit of *catenaccio* is all tied up with the Italian mentality. Even now, Italian footballers go into a game not wanting to concede goals; their first instinct is not to lose the game. We go into a game wanting to win it. This Inter side was the extreme manifestation of that Italian mentality, and I suppose Celtic were the extreme version of the British attack-attack-attack mentality. In reality, the best teams in the world, certainly in the modern game, play with a combination of both philosophies.

The Italian system invited pressure but Inter were happy to take it. But I always wondered, when you have the *catenaccio* defence and your mind is set in that way, how you change mentally to a positive frame of mind when you let in a goal and have to attack. That's what happened here. After all the pressure the Italian defence finally gave way in the sixty-third minute. After that Celtic continued to pile forward and Inter continued to sit back. It was as if one side was stuck in attack mode and the other in defence mode and neither could switch to anything else.

I think the Italians found it so hard against England in Rome, trying to qualify for the World Cup in France in 1997 because of their defensive mentality. For once Italy simply had to win, they had to come out and attack, while England were quite happy to sit back and defend. It was a complete role reversal. So often England have gone into this kind of game knowing that they must beat Italy. They would struggle to break down the blue-shirted defence and the Italians would pinch it 1–0. But this time England just bottled them up and made them look ordinary. The Italians just didn't seem to know how to commit themselves to all-out attack.

Defeat against Celtic was a crushing blow to Herrera's 'invincible' Inter. It was followed by failure to retain the Italian title and defeat in the semi-final of the *Coppa Italia* against Second Division opposition. It was the beginning of the end for *catenaccio*. Celtic had proved that the Inter defence could be breached. But Herrera refused to accept that tactics were responsible, instead he blamed the sweeper Picchi for Inter's crash. Picchi was soon sold to lower league club Varese, where he claimed: 'When things go right it is always Herrera's brilliant planning. When things go wrong, it is always the players who are to blame.'

I think the truth is that Inter Milan were made for Celtic. When Celtic equalised Inter's whole gameplan was destroyed. Psychologically the game had totally changed and Celtic were already in an attacking rhythm. So when they scored again, the Italians never looked like getting back in it. While McNeill and Clark were solid as a rock at the back and Murdoch and Auld helped them out when they had to, this Celtic side was clearly too positive an attacking force for Inter.

We can talk about tactics until we are blue in the face – I frequently do – but at the end of the day the only reason that Celtic could break down this defence was because they had great players. As teams didn't play offside in those days and the play was spread across the whole length of the pitch, the good players had more time and more space. That's why I believe in those days the better team won more often than they do today. Nowadays poorer teams can stifle the play and in the modern game they have closed down the space for the good player. But believe you me, on 25 May 1967 the better team won.

CHAPTER 7
Defensive
Tactics

• •

I went for a month on loan to Notts County in 1987 and got my first and only taste of what it's like to play at the back. I played a few games at centre back in a back four and, to be quite honest, I found it comfortable. I certainly didn't think it was as difficult as playing centre forward, because at the back everything is in front of you, you can see the whole picture.

Playing in defence is all about sensing danger and being in the right place to deal with that danger. It's about reading the game. Playing up front is more instinctive, more off the cuff. Having said that, of course, a great defender is as big an asset as a great goalscorer to any team. A saving tackle or clearance off the line is as valuable as a goal.

I've already talked about the most obvious and most important defensive tactic, namely the offside trap. Whether a team decides to push up and hold the line or drop slightly deeper and defend more traditionally is one of the biggest decisions a coach must make when setting out his gameplan.

When I started playing in the mid-1970s teams were far more conscious of holding the line, pushing up and playing offside (figure 34). It became rife. The reason this happened, I think, is because poorer teams who, if the game was stretched like it was in 1966 would have been found out, had to come up with ways of stopping their opponents. One way was to squeeze the play and push up so that skilful opponents had less time, less space and thus less opportunity to influence the game. As a forward I used to hate playing against this

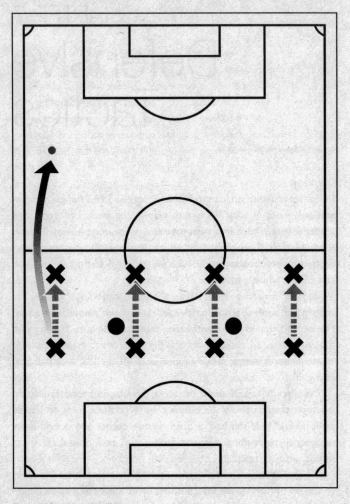

Figure 34: Pushing up for offside

kind of team. It was terrible. I used to spend half the match running towards my own goal.

Arsenal's success under George Graham, when they won the League Championship in 1989 and 1991, was built on a defence which played offside as well as any team I have ever seen. With a back four of Lee Dixon at right back, Tony Adams and Steve Bould in the middle and Nigel Winterburn at left back, they were the masters of the trap. It was not so much that they were great individual players, but that they were so well organised, so well drilled, that they always timed the movement of the line upfield to perfection. The image of Tony Adams with his arm raised, appealing for the offside flag, is one that is indelibly etched on the minds of any football fans who ever saw this team.

Terry Venables has a tactic which all the teams he's been manager of have used. QPR had it, Tottenham had it and England had it. When they were defending on the edge of the box, as soon as the opposition wide man made his move to come in with the ball the back four stepped up. Bang. Five yards. Everyone offside (figure 35). It's a move and a tactic that Terry has used right through his career. When the player comes infield that's the trigger to push up.

A good manager, of course, will try to counter these tactics. If I was manager of a team playing against one of Terry's sides I would tell my forwards that when Terry's back four pushes out they should push out with them. They have all got to come out to stay onside. Then I would tell my wide man either to keep the ball himself and go for goal or slide a little ball through for a midfield player making a run from deep. That's the way to beat it.

Nowadays things have changed quite a bit because of the amendments to the offside rule. Players are now deemed to be onside if they are level with the last defender and players who are running back (away from goal) are not offside, so playing an offside trap is a much more risky game. Even with the rule changes, however, you will still see a Premiership match these days with both defences pushed right up and the game squeezed into the twenty yards either side of the halfway line.

On top of good old offside, though, there are many facets to the

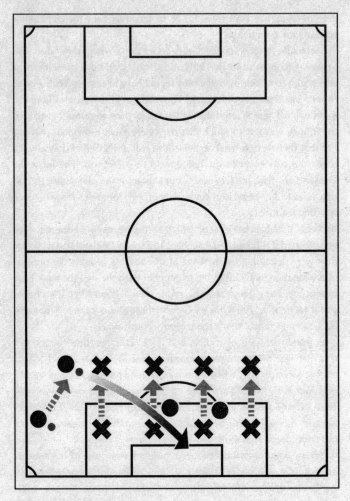

Figure 35: Terry Venables' offside tactic

art of defending which – because if they're working well might result simply in a forward player having to pass back to a midfielder or attempt a shot from distance that soars over the bar – go unnoticed.

Some of these, of course, are highly illegal. The art of shirt-pulling, pushing and holding without being spotted by the referee are all part of the defenders' repertoire. I think in my day it wasn't as bad as it is now, defenders were a bit more honest, but then these days forwards get so much protection from referees that defenders are only trying to redress the balance. When I was a player I always knew that, as the main striker, I had to expect what I called a 'welcome to the game' tackle from my marker. If, in the first ten minutes, I was standing near the halfway line with my back to goal and the ball came to me, I would brace myself for a crunching tackle from behind. I knew it was coming. The idea was to unsettle me and make me afraid of the next challenge, although I like to think it took more than that to unsettle me.

Defenders can't do that now, because referees are so much stricter. Fifteen years ago you would have to assault someone to get sent off whereas if you so much as breathe on a striker these days you're off. You simply can't get away with things on or off the ball so much now because there are television cameras all over the place. Defenders have therefore had to adjust to the modern game more than anyone.

Of course, there are still many perfectly legal tactics that a good defender will use against another player to limit his effectiveness in front of goal. I think people who played against me would probably have tried to keep me on the right-hand side of the pitch and on my right foot because they knew I was so much stronger on the left. A defender might encourage me to go onto my right side by positioning himself in front of me but slightly to my left, blocking the route which I favoured and inviting me down the right.

I'm sure that's what good defenders do when Alan Shearer is tearing towards them with the ball at his feet. I know if Alan Shearer was coming through on me I would try and force him inside leftish, because I know he's weaker on his left than he is on his right. I would do my utmost to stop him turning onto his right foot.

Defenders can do this by positioning themselves in the right place and staying on their feet. Great defenders are the ones that don't go to ground very much. You don't often see them sliding in to make tackles or stretching a despairing leg out because their positioning and reading of the game is so good that they don't need to. If you jump into a tackle then you are committing yourself to winning the ball at all costs, because if you don't win it you will be flat on your back on the deck and the attacking player will be clear of you. That is why getting into the right position and jockeying – standing up in front of the ball, keeping on your toes, staying perfectly balanced so that you can move whichever way the attacker does – is so important.

In a situation where a defender is standing up in front of an attacker, both are trying to force the other into doing something he doesn't want to do. The attacker wants the defender to dive in so that he can skip past and get away while the defender wants the attacker to make a move one way or the other so that he can pick his moment to get his foot in. That's why when you watch a game of football you always hear coaches shouting 'stand up, stand up' to defenders.

In his prime, the great central defender Bobby Moore, of West Ham and England, was the master of jockeying. He would stay on his feet when a striker was running at him and wait for the chance to pounce. By concentrating on the ball, by reading what the striker was about to do, usually it would just take a perfectly timed boot to nick the ball away. In this way, if he didn't win the ball cleanly, he would still be on his feet and able to carry on defending.

Jockeying is particularly important in the modern game because forwards have so much pace and many teams play a counter-attacking style. Defenders need to be able to keep their feet whilst running back and jockeying a forward for maybe thirty yards or so. They may not be able to break up the whole attack, but just by staying on their feet and keeping themselves between the ball and the goal they are buying their team some time, allowing other players to get back and help.

Say you are Lee Dixon, Arsenal's right back. Imagine your team has just had a corner and your centre backs, Adams and Bould, have gone up the field for it. The ball is cleared, and suddenly you're up against Ryan Giggs on the break. It's one on one so if he gets past you it's a certain goal. You've just got to stop him from knocking it past you and sprinting by, and the only way you can do that is by jockeying him. If you do it for forty yards, you halt his progress for perhaps five seconds and that's enough time for Adams and Bould to get back. The danger isn't gone, but it's a lot less than when Giggs is one mistimed tackle away from being clean through on goal.

As a defender, you have a choice on the occasions when your opponent does get level with the eighteen-yard box. You must decide whether to send him wide and then deal with the cross, or turn him inside onto what should be his weaker foot and let him run across the length of the penalty area. Defenders do this by choosing where they position themselves in front of the player running at them. By standing alongside him they block his route inside, forcing him to go down the line. Alternatively, if they stand in front of him he has to come inside.

Now I would say 'send him wide', because there's only one ball coming in then and that's a cross. If you have a couple of decent centre backs you should be confident of defending a cross (figure 36). The reason I think it's safer to send him wide is that if you turn him inside you're still open to a cross, but you're also open to him shifting it across square to someone coming in from twenty-five yards for a shot or even sliding a little diagonal ball through your back four for a runner (figure 37). To me, one moment of danger is easier to deal with than three.

Then again, if your opponents have got someone like Les Ferdinand or Duncan Ferguson charging into the box then maybe you are better off sending the player inside. A decent cross is the last thing you want to have to deal with. People who played against me would have tried to send the wide player inside, because one thing they didn't want him to do was go down the line and cross it and have me climbing all over them.

When I was playing teams would probably have sat down before the game and thought of ways to stop crosses from coming into the box. They would have thought that if they stopped the supply they would stop me. To stop a player getting a cross in, one option you have is 'double banking'. This means that you make sure you have your wide midfield man and your full back going against the opposi-

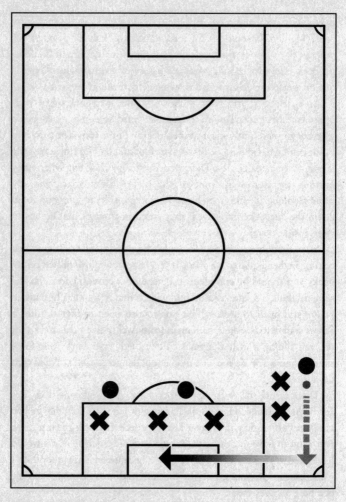

Figure 36: In this situation the defenders are favourites to come out on top. The attacking player, sent wide, has only one option, the cross

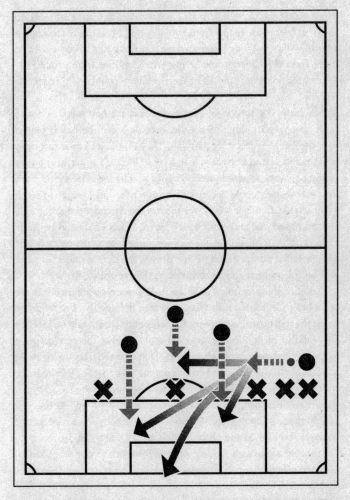

Figure 37: The attacking player, allowed to come inside, has four options to create a scoring chance

tion's wide man, the danger man when it comes to getting crosses into the box (figure 38). Teams would obviously work at this in the knowledge that if a cross was going to come in it was going to come in from deep, from the halfway line or just over, and not from around the edge of the box where myself or Graeme Sharp could really attack the ball.

Similarly, if someone is very, very quick, the best tactic is not to push up trying to play him offside, because when the ball is played over the top he will just fly past you. The best thing to do is just drop off him and defend normally. You have to look at the players you are playing against. If people were playing against me they would push up as far as they could because I was never the quickest, and there's a fair chance that if it went over the top the defender would be able to turn round and stay with me. Whereas if Les Ferdinand or Andy Cole, with their phenomenal pace, are pushed up to the halfway line and the ball is pumped over the top there is less chance that a defender will be able to turn and catch them, so they've got to drop off.

Another thing teams would do if they were playing against me would be to let me have the ball at my feet, because I was never going to get the ball down, turn, twist, beat three and smash one in. I wasn't that kind of player. I wasn't a Zola or a Juninho. I'm sure before a game my opponents would have said, 'Don't get too tight up his backside, let him have the ball when he's got his back to goal, let him bring it down on the floor, because you know he's not going to beat you. And if he does turn, make sure it's onto his right foot.' Again, you can do that just by the way you position your body. As a manager or a coach you look at the players you are up against closely, trying to see their strengths and weaknesses and instructing your defenders to play accordingly.

Not all defending, however, is done by defenders. Something that is often overlooked is that defending begins from the front. You look at teams like Manchester United and when they haven't got the ball the defending begins with people like Cole and Sheringham up front. Defending from the front is something you can do only if you have got two willing strikers. I think you need two – it's not something you can do with one. We used to do it at Everton a lot because Graeme

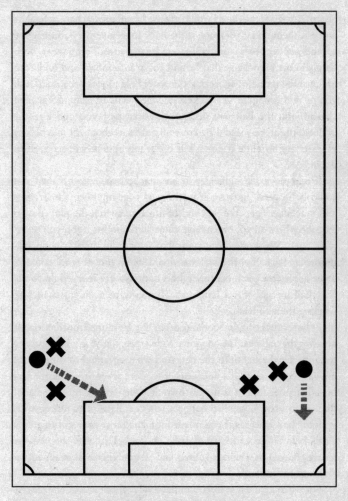

Figure 38: Double banking. How not to do it (left) and how to do it properly (right)

Sharp, Adrian Heath and I would always be willing to chase defenders and put them under pressure. If the back four have the ball then you go and put whoever's on the ball under pressure. You have to do it happy in the knowledge that behind you your midfield and back four are pushing up tight, squeezing the space behind you because, if not, you're just going to get picked off. You will be running around chasing and the ball will just get threaded past you and into the midfield (figures 39 and 40). You will have run about for maybe fifty yards trying to close it down but the whole system will have fallen down.

If one player, a midfielder or an attacker, switches off then you could be in total disarray. If just one of your opponents is left free and that player gets the ball and has time to switch the play and go left side where all your men have come across to the right, you're left wide open. We worked it very well at Everton in that if the opposition's left back had the ball we would make sure that he couldn't come across the pitch because all his options were marked up so the only ball he had was a long one. That gave us a decent chance of winning the ball back.

I was brought up in Scotland defending from the front because if you win the ball near the opponent's goal then you've got less distance to go to get the ball into the net. And what I wanted to do most of all was score a goal. It's much easier to score when you nick the ball off a defender than it is if your own defender wins it on the edge of his penalty area. When that happens you've still got to go ninety yards with the ball whereas if you're a front man you've only got to go ten yards before you can have a strike on goal. That was the way we always played at Dundee United and Aston Villa and it suited me down to the ground.

But when I tried it at international level it didn't work. The players were too good and they had the ability simply to pass it round me or beat me with a bit of skill. I kept on getting picked off and the manager, Jock Stein, told me: 'Andy, at international level what we do is drop off to the halfway line, everybody.' When the players' skills are generally so much better you cannot bank on the defenders making the mistakes that make defending from the front worthwhile.

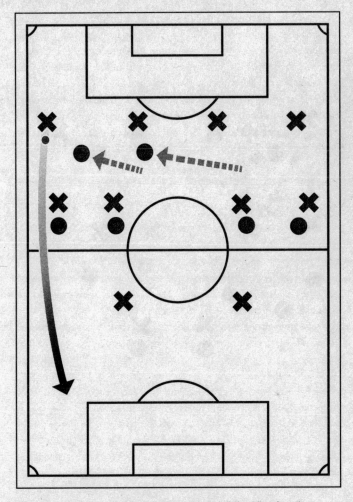

Figure 39: Defending from the front. By both attacking the ball, the strikers force the opposition full back into playing a hopeful long ball

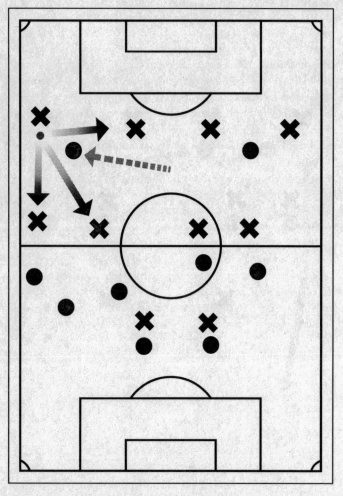

Figure 40: If only one striker goes to the ball and his midfielders don't get tight onto the opposition's midfield, it is easy for the full back to pick out a pass

At international level the theory is that your opponents cannot score from their own half if you're all back behind the ball. If you're only defending half a pitch then there's less space for the opposition to exploit. You can set your stall out, have your back four set, get your midfield four set – both close together – and let your strikers work them across the halfway line. That's a safer policy away from home and if you think the other team is better than you.

The art of defending, either from the front or at the back, is all about studying the players you are up against. The teams I played in always used to close down the opposition back four and leave the poorest player at the back with the ball. We would decide in advance which of the back four players was weakest with the ball at his feet and when it came to him you wouldn't put any pressure on him but you would mark everyone else tightly instead. The idea was that because he was not a great passer of the ball there was more chance of him giving it back to you. It worked well.

For nearly twenty-five years as a pro defenders were my arch enemies, but there weren't many who I didn't feel that I could beat. And fortunately for the game of football, the totally unbeatable defence has not yet evolved.

CHAPTER 8
Attacking Tactics

● ●

If you asked people who watched me during my playing career what my tactics were as a striker they would probably tell you that my main one was to shut my eyes, stick out my elbows and dive head first towards the ball. Although I was strong and brave and not bad in the air, I like to think there was a bit more to my game than that. I was no Romario or Cantona, but I don't think I would have been able to achieve what I did without a half-decent footballing brain.

As a striker I was brought up playing in a partnership of two forwards. It was very much the way to play in the days when I grew up in the mid-1970s and the duo that everyone used to think of and look up to in those days was Toshack and Keegan at Liverpool. Toshack was the big man, strong, powerful and good in the air, and Keegan, more mobile and skilful, would feed off his little headers and knock-downs.

Playing as a duo means playing as a unit. You've got to be constantly talking. You've got to tell your partner where to run to pull defenders out of position and create space for yourself and when to attack the near post or pull out into the space in front of the defence. You must be constantly close and never more than about twenty yards apart.

Playing as part of a front two is very much built on knowing where your partner is when you are in certain situations. For instance, when I was at Villa I was fortunate enough to play alongside Brian Little. We worked on the theory that I was the centre forward, the target man. I was the Toshack-type player, the big player who would win the ball in the air and try to knock it down or flick it on for Brian who was smaller, quicker and more skilful than me. He was the Keegan. Brian could receive the ball brilliantly and control it, and he would float around me. Although I was mobile, I never had the skill or ability, when I got the ball wide or when I got the ball deep, to turn and beat men. So Brian would feed off me when the ball came up to us, and then when he got it I would look for him to do something clever – either to provide himself with a scoring chance or to put me into a scoring position with a cross or a little through ball.

One team that plays with a classic front two in the Premiership is Blackburn Rovers with Chris Sutton and Kevin Gallacher; just as they did when they won the championship in 1995 when they had the so-called 'SAS' strike force of Shearer and Sutton. When the ball is played up to Sutton and Gallacher they almost play as a separate team, using little one-twos, flicks and little chips to try and carve out an opening. You can build up a relationship with a striker that is almost telepathic, but the understanding comes from playing together and working hard on the training ground.

We had this kind of understanding at Villa. It became second nature. For instance whenever Brian had the ball in a wide position on the edge of the box, I knew that as soon as he knocked the ball half a yard in front of him he was just about to cross it in to the near post. By looking at his feet I knew when to start my run into the box, and he knew exactly where I would be to meet his cross without having to look up and see where I was. I knew he was going to play it to the near post and he knew I would be attacking the near post, so we had an advantage over the defenders because we knew what was happening before they did. Obviously it didn't always work, but the amount of goals he created for me with that little move was quite incredible.

That kind of understanding comes because you are good, intelligent footballers, but you do have to work at it in training. You play practice matches and 'shadow football', where you don't play against anyone but just take the ball into certain situations on the pitch and go round the team working out the best positions for various players to take up, what runs should be made and who should make them.

We did a lot of this work, but primarily our success was due to the fact that he was a good player and I was intelligent enough to work out where I should be to capitalise on his skill.

There are certain other little moves that we would always try to play. Basically, we were trying to exploit the space behind the full back. If you can get space in that area you have the opposition in serious trouble because the defence is going to be back-pedalling and you have the option of shooting, firing in a cross or laying the ball back for someone on the edge of the box. It's a crucial area. If you're a striker and you run into that area your marker is simply going to go with you, so even if you get the ball there's no space. So we always tried to get our wide man to attract the full back further up the pitch. The wide man would do this by dropping deep to receive the ball, hoping that the full back would advance to challenge him. Then the striker on that side of the pitch would show for the ball. If the defender marking him went with him, which was what you hoped for, there would be a huge hole where the full back and centre back had been. So, as soon as the centre back pushed up to follow the first striker, the second would make a run into that space. The ball would be played almost straight away into this channel and the striker would be away (figure 41). He would have the ball in acres of space in one of the most dangerous areas of the pitch.

But that wasn't our only move. If the ball was around the halfway line on one side of the pitch and I was the furthest striker from the ball Brian would show for the ball, moving up ten yards towards the player in possession, taking one of the centre backs with him. But as soon as he made this run the player with the ball would ignore him and play a diagonal ball up to me in the air. And as soon as that ball was played Brian would spin round and run back towards goal, hopefully getting to the edge of the box ahead of his marker just as I knocked the ball down into his path (figure 42).

These are the types of things that you can work at as a centre forward. They were almost set plays. We didn't need a call to let everyone know what was happening because everyone knew what to do and when we were going to do it. Of course, you play off the cuff most of the time, but there are times when set tactics come into play

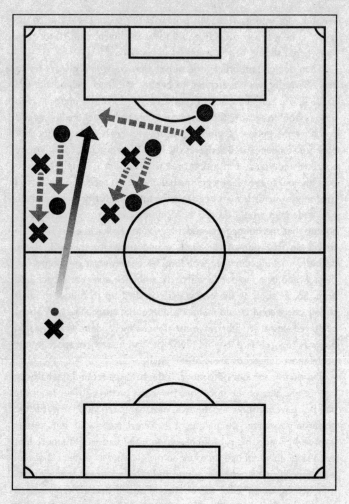

Figure 41: Creating space behind the full back

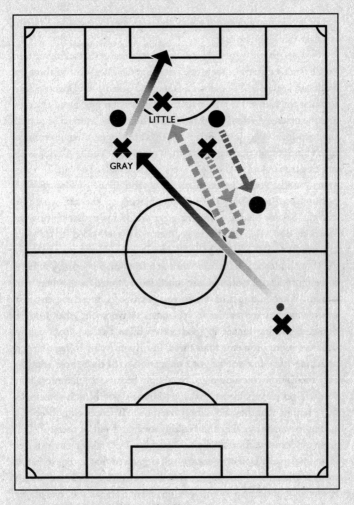

Figure 42: Drawing the centre back out of position

which are so ingrained in the way the team works that you do them without thinking about it.

Two up front is probably still the most common attacking system in the British game but there are other options. We went to three up front for a while at Villa when a young lad called John Deehan came through the ranks. He was a striker who was on fire in the reserves and the manager, Ron Saunders, wanted him in the team so he played three up front with John, Brian and myself. Playing three up front is much harder than playing with two. It means that you're playing with one target man and two wide players on either side. To make sure the system works you must be much more rigid about sticking to your position because having three players playing off the cuff would be chaotic. So, for example, the manager would insist that if we were attacking down the right the target man and the left-sided striker went into the box to attack the ball (figure 43).

Three up front is harder to work as a front man because you have to be more disciplined. You are much more limited as to where you can go. When you just have two you are always interchanging, it is less regimented and harder for defenders to work out what you are doing. If the movement is good then I think two up front causes defences more problems than three, but if you want to be a strong attacking force but you've got average forwards then three is probably the option you would go for, simply because it guarantees that you will get players in the box. Joe Kinnear's Wimbledon sometimes do it, hoping that they will simply overpower defences with three big, strong forwards hustling and bustling away in front of them.

In modern-day football the hardest thing about playing as a striker is finding space. Defences are so well organised that trying to break them down can be like banging your head against a brick wall which is why a lot of teams play with one up and one off. That is, one player pushed right up on the centre backs and the other playing slightly deeper in what has become known as 'the hole'. Look at Manchester United with Cole as the front man and Sheringham slightly withdrawn, look at England with Sheringham in the hole again and Shearer ahead of him.

The theory here is that when teams lose the ball they make sure

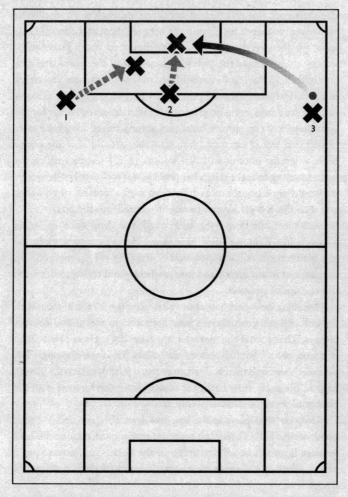

Figure 43: If you play three up front, two of your strikers must attack any ball played into the box by the third one

that their back line and their midfield line are as close as possible to each other, so there's hardly any gap between them and effectively no space for the strikers to work in. The idea is to find a player who, when you don't have the ball, just drops out of the attack and gets himself behind the team's midfield. He now has space and can either run at the defence or try to open it up by playing crafty little through balls or get things going by playing balls into dangerous areas for the wide players to run onto. When Eric Cantona played for Manchester United you would often find him scurrying around near the centre circle when the opposition's defence was tightly set, picking up the ball and trying to make things happen. He was still a striker, however. He would often begin a move from deep with a moment of brilliance and then finish it off himself having thundered into the box.

Sometimes the deep-lying striker will not drop back as far as someone like Cantona might have done. He will try to work in the gap between the midfield and attack, dropping off his marker – by slipping out of the attack and into midfield – and trying to draw the defence out of position.

One thing defenders hate above all is players who run at them with the ball. All the great players have been able to run at and commit players. That's what the player in 'the hole' does. He is able to turn and run with the ball before defenders are even moving. The defender's decision then is, 'Do I go to him?' If he does he risks leaving gaps at the back. If he backs off he may leave the forward with the chance to smash it in from twenty yards.

Anybody who plays in the hole has invariably got ability and is good on the ball. There's no point putting a hard man in the hole because he won't be able to influence the game. You have to put a player who's got a range of passing, a good football brain and a decent shot.

Playing just one up front is a choice that few teams make. If you are playing this method you need to have people from midfield who are going to support the attack very quickly. You need to have good athletes, people who can get from the midfield to the front and back again very quickly and you need good, creative players in the midfield who can make things happen. Then you have got to get your team to play through the midfield and pass the ball from back to front. There's no point in knocking endless long balls to a player on his own up front. It's too big a job for him to protect the ball and hold it up until support arrives. By the time that happens the opposition defence will be in place. It's a system played by teams who like to pass the ball – West Ham sometimes play it in difficult away games with John Hartson on his own up front – and it's the support play around the front man which is crucial to making it work.

Playing on your own up front is a strange role for a striker because he becomes more of a creator around the edge of the box than a finisher. He must receive the ball and then try to feed the midfielders who are running from deep. I remember when Terry Venables was England manager he tried to play with one up front in what became known as the Christmas tree formation (figure 44). He had Alan Shearer on his own at the top of the tree and Alan found it very difficult. I remember him saying that he might only get one chance a game because he spent most of the time as an outlet, receiving the ball and holding it up until he got support from other players. He had to be so focused on being a build-up player that he found it tough to score goals and he went about twelve games without hitting the target. However, I think Shearer can play this way and that England did have skilful enough players to make it work but, as I think Terry realised, if you've got a goalscorer like Shearer in your squad then this system is a waste of talent.

One up front is very much a system to use in a big away game, perhaps in Europe, when you know you're going to be under the cosh so you want to bring an extra man into midfield to tighten everything up. If I was a manager this is certainly the only kind of situation when I would use the system. There are only certain players who can play as lone striker. They need to be strong enough to play with their backs to goal and have good enough control to keep the ball when it comes to them. I'm thinking of players like Shearer and Mark Hughes, not players whose main asset is that they are pure finishers like Michael Owen and Robbie Fowler of Liverpool.

Within any system, there are different ways of playing. A manager not only has to decide how many players he wants in midfield and

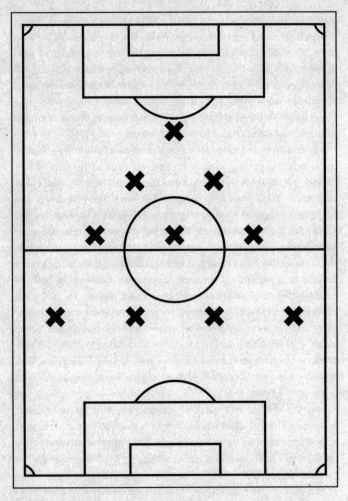

Figure 44: Terry Venables' 'Christmas Tree' formation

how many up front, but also exactly how offensively or defensively these players should play. I was always a great believer in having three of your midfield players involved in the attack when you were in the last third of the pitch and that's how I would have played it had I ever become a manager. If the ball was with my left winger and my left back and the cross was coming in, I would expect my two front men, one of my central midfielders and my right-sided player all to be in the box. That would have been my demand. Then I would have one midfield player on the edge of the box to pick up anything that broke loose (figure 45).

Now that's a pretty attacking philosophy and one which I would have worked on during training. When the ball was played up to the front man I would have wanted three of my players going past him towards goal (one right in front of him, and one either side of him). I would have wanted the other striker and two midfielders running past him, and another midfield player dropping behind him, so whichever way the ball came off him, either intentionally or not, there would be someone there to pick up the pieces (figure 46).

You have to trigger in the players' minds what you want from them. A lot of managers, when the ball is played up to a target man, would only have support players. By that I mean players sitting in behind the striker who would look to get the ball played back to them and then build from there (figure 47). My option is much more attacking and there are plenty of coaches who would never dream of playing anything so adventurous. I think I'm right in saying, however, that you have to score goals to win football matches.

As well as the type of forward system you play, there are all sorts of individual tactics you can play as a striker to try to get one up on your opponent. For instance, I was never one who wanted to go deep too often. I didn't want to come back, get the ball and have to turn and beat players. That wasn't my game. I wanted the ball played over the top of the back four so that I could run onto it. So for about the first ten minutes of a game, I would go short for every ball. I would make a move back towards the midfielder with the ball, receive it at my feet and lay it off simply to someone else. That would draw my defender closer. Now if I had just run forward every time, from the

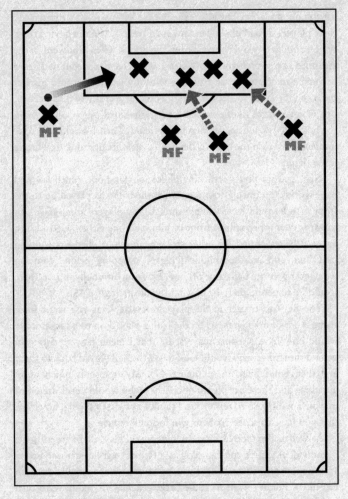

Figure 45: Two midfielders go into the box to support the strikers as the ball is crossed in, meaning there are four players attacking the ball in the box

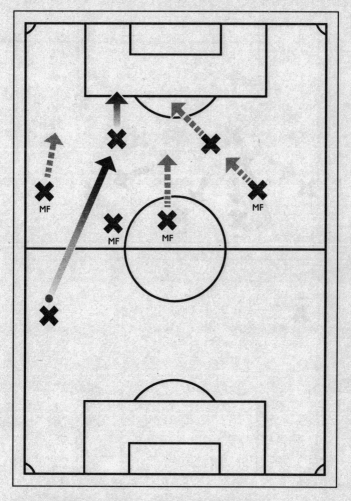

Figure 46: Midfielders supporting their striker in an attack-minded system

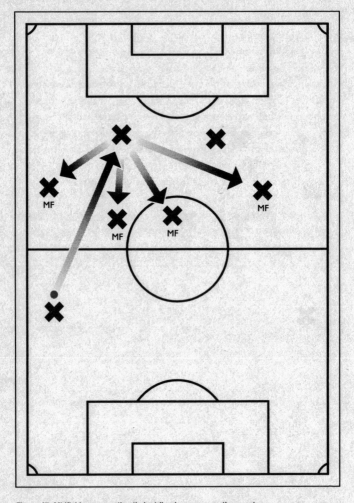

Figure 47: Midfielders supporting their striker in a more cautious system

very first whistle, my defender would have backed off me and I would never have beaten him to a ball over the top. He would simply turn and be ahead of me all the way to the ball. I didn't have the pace to win a race when the defender had a two-yard start. But if I could attract him deep for ten minutes, and get him to come close to me because he thought that was where I was going every time, then the next time the ball came over the top I might have had a chance. I would take a couple of steps towards the ball as if I was going deep again, then suddenly spin and start running the other way. Hopefully the defender would be so close to me that I would be able to spin round and get ahead of him in the race for the ball which had just been played over the top.

So next time anyone says, 'that Andy Gray was nothing but brute strength and commitment,' you can tell them about some of the finer points of my game.

CHAPTER 9
Brazil 1970

●●●●●●●●●●●●●●●●●●●●●●●●

BRAZIL 4 ITALY 1
21 June 1970 (World Cup Final)
Azteca Stadium, Mexico. Attendance: 107,000

Brazil: (4–2–4)

Felix

Alberto   Brito   Piazza   Everaldo

Clodoaldo   Gerson

Jairzinho   Pele   Tostao   Rivelino

Italy: Albertosi, Burgnigh, Cera, Rosato, Facchetti, Bertini, Mazzola, De Sisti, Domenghini, Boninsegna, Riva

The question people were asking before the game was how long could Italy's famous defence hold out against Brazil's awesome attack, and Pele answered that one in the eighteenth minute. His powerful downward header not only gave Brazil the lead in the searing Azteca heat, it also made him the first person in football history to score in two World Cup Finals (he got two in 1958). After that the Brazilians continued to surge forward but their attacking exuberance left them exposed at the back and when Clodoaldo carelessly backheeled the ball to Boninsegna on the edge of his own box, the Italian striker gratefully accepted the gift and made it 1–1. From then on the battle between two of football's heavyweights was immense. Brazil attacked, Italy defended and tried to break away, and the deadlock remained. Until the sixty-sixth minute, that is, when the forty cigarettes-a-day Brazilian midfielder Gerson danced through a couple of Italian challenges and fired the ball home. Five minutes later it was 3–1, Jairzinho bundling the ball past Albertosi in the Italian goal. Italy were dead and buried. It was now time for Brazil to really turn on the style; it was all one-touch passes and little flicks. Eventually the ball came to Jairzinho who slipped it to Pele on the edge of the box. Pele spotted Carlos Alberto steaming towards goal on the right and simply rolled the ball into his path. The Brazilian captain didn't even have to break stride before thumping the ball joyously into the corner to make it 4–1 and secure the Jules Rimet Trophy for Brazil for keeps (until someone stole it from the Brazilian FA, that is).

If Britain is the home of football then Brazil is where you will find its soul. A nation renowned for its very own brand of flamboyant, daring and, at times, breathtaking football, Brazil has a place in the hearts of all football supporters. People say Brazil play football the way football was meant to be played, but back in the early days of the game no one could have imagined that it was possible to play like some of the great Brazilian sides have done.

The team that won the World Cup in 1970, featuring the likes of Jairzinho, Rivelino, Carlos Alberto, Gerson, Tostao, and, of course, the king himself, Pele, is considered by many to be the greatest football team ever to set foot on grass. In the searing heat and lung-destroying altitude of Mexico they danced to a record third World Cup triumph with play that took the game into another dimension. Stroking the ball majestically about the pitch, launching electric attacks with sudden upshifts in gear, shooting from just about anywhere and doing tricks with the ball like they were playing 'three and in' on Copacabana Beach, Brazil were irresistible, and the world, watching live and in colour for the first time, fell in love.

Perhaps it is the world's love affair with Brazilian football, however, which has slightly clouded our view of their game. Ever since that 1970 tournament we have over-romanticised them. As the game has got faster, more commercial and more tactical we have looked to Brazil to provide us with a flamboyant two-fingered salute to rigid formations, offside traps and hard fought 1–0 wins. But this does Brazilian football an injustice because, although there's no doubt that their teams have usually played with unbounded enthusiasm and breathtaking flair, they are not as tactically naive as they are often portrayed.

Brazil have always played attacking football. It's in the blood, it's part of the national psyche. It's a reputation which was forged for the first time on the world stage in the 1950 World Cup held in Brazil, when they reached the final. On that occasion tactical naivety probably cost them their first ever world title. Beaten 2–1 by the tough, experienced Uruguayans (in front of the biggest crowd ever to watch a football match – 199,589 – in the Maracana Stadium in Rio) their individually more gifted team was unable to match the collective quality of their South American rivals. Eight years later, however, they showed that they had learned their lesson.

In 1958 Brazil arrived in Sweden with two secret weapons. The first was a 17-year-old called Edson Arantes do Nascimento – better known as Pele – and the second was a previously unheard of 4–2–4 formation. The biggest tactical development since Herbert Chapman devised the 'WM' formation, 4–2–4 was to revolutionise football. Brazil are always remembered for their outrageous attacking play but their first World Cup victory had its foundations in their super-tight four-man defence (figure 48).

The revolutionary back line featured two centre backs in the middle who marked zones instead of particular players. Alongside them, the two full backs pushed tight onto the opposition wingers to restrict what was in those days the main route of supply for virtually every team. In front of the defence there were two central midfielders whose job was to build attacks and four forwards whose job was to do the bit that everyone knows the Brazilians for...sticking the ball in the back of the net.

Teams found it very difficult to break down this defence as their strikers were not used to playing against a flat line of defenders and were constantly flagged for offside. The flat back four had been invented. Pele scored twice in the 5–2 final win over Sweden, and

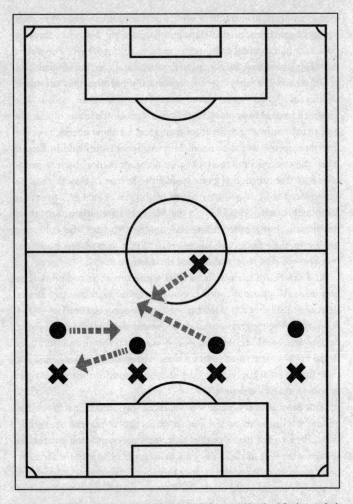

Figure 48: Brazil's revolutionary flat back four. Instead of man marking the defenders marked zones, retaining their shape at all times. When attackers went deep they were picked up by the midfield

Brazil had won their first World Cup. It was a triumph achieved with tremendously talented, flamboyant attacking play, but it had its roots in a tactical masterstroke.

Playing with exactly the same system Brazil won the World Cup again in 1962, beating Chile 3–1 in front of their own fans in Santiago, although by now pretty much every international side was playing the same formation. In 1966 the teams Brazil came up against realised the only way to stop them was to kick them off the pitch. In their opening group match against Portugal they were brutally put out of their stride. Pele was injured and for once the mighty Brazil couldn't play themselves out of trouble. They were knocked out in the first round for the first and only time since 1934.

In 1970 the Brazilian FA left nothing to chance. The players were withdrawn from club soccer in Brazil, where it was not uncommon for teams to be asked to play four times a week, and holed up in a training camp four months before the Mexico finals. Consequently, just before the tournament started Pele was able to announce that he felt properly fit for the first time in years. Before the finals one Brazilian official said: 'We have timed everything to come to a peak at precisely the right moment. We are ready to explode.'

I remember sitting at home with my jaw wide open watching Brazil in the 1970 World Cup. They were astonishing. This must have been the most attacking team ever to go into a World Cup. It was like the official said, they were ready to explode. Each player wanted the ball badly and whenever he got it, whether he was the centre back or the centre forward, he wanted to go forward. The passing was as precise as you will ever see, the pace was frightening and the invention and imagination – let alone the finishing – were frankly unbelievable.

They played their 4–2–4 system but in reality it was far more attacking than it looks on paper. Whereas in 1958 the back four had hardly crossed the halfway line, in 1970 they took far more risks. Carlos Alberto, the team's captain and right back, must have spent more time around the edge of his opponents' penalty area than he ever did on the edge of his own. He was a constant attacking menace, a brilliant, incisive player, and when one of the Brazilian central midfielders pushed up as well, as they often did (usually Gerson), teams would be faced with an incredible yellow wave, a six-man attack with pure Brazilian skill running right through it. It did mean that they were shaky at the back at times, but that didn't mean that they were disorganised. They must have made a conscious decision to go for all-out attack, confident that they had the ability to score more goals than any other team.

The only side that they were frightened of during the 1970 tournament, Pele said, was England. The two sides met in the early rounds in what many believed was a precursor to the final and that was the only time when Brazil showed any real semblance of caution. Brazil won the game 1–0 with a goal from Jairzinho, but it was the only occasion when they showed that they could be disciplined and organised when necessary. I'm not suggesting they played like George Graham's Leeds United, but they showed that they could pick their moments to be adventurous and temper their attacking instincts by keeping possession and trying to exert a grip on the game.

The match against England was the only game of the tournament in which Brazil didn't concede a goal. In the other group games they demolished Czechoslovakia, scoring four – it would have been five had Pele's incredible shot from the halfway line not landed inches wide of the post – but let one in. Against Romania they conceded two as the defence was exposed by the urge to attack. Against Peru in the quarter-finals they let in two more but scored four, and in the semi-finals a defensive mix-up between Brito and goalkeeper Felix let Uruguay take the lead before Brazil restored order with a 3–1 victory.

In the final they met Italy whose mean *catenaccio* defence was expected to provide the sternest test yet for this explosive Brazilian front line. The question being asked of the Italians before the game was would their traditionally cautious approach offer enough of a threat to the Brazilian defence which had proved itself breachable, mainly because of the number of men they threw forward. The feeling before the game was that it wouldn't be easy for Brazil to win the trophy for a record third time. Italy were looking to achieve the same feat and it had been deemed that whoever won would get the famous Jules Rimet trophy for keeps. In the end, attack triumphed over defence, but it wasn't as clear-cut a victory as the 4–1 scoreline suggests.

Brazil lined up in their usual way. They had a back four of Carlos Alberto, Brito, Piazza and Everaldo, two central midfielders in Gerson and Clodoaldo and then an awesome front line of four out and out forwards – Rivelino, Tostao, Pele and Jairzinho. Rivelino was on the left but because he was fond of drifting inside he certainly wasn't a winger, and Jairzinho was exactly the same on the right. Then they had Pele and Tostao in the middle. Tostao played slightly ahead of Pele, holding the ball up superbly and often turning provider for the great man. All four were incredibly quick – in both thought and deed – and they all had more skill than you would have thought humanly possible. Defending against them must have been a frightening prospect even if, like the Italians, you had a four-man defence plus a sweeper.

In central midfield Clodoaldo was the holding midfielder while Gerson was the playmaker. He would receive the ball, link up with the attack and generally keep the whole team ticking over. He was a marvellous player and the unsung hero of the team, and he would often join the attack to effectively make it five up front. And then there was Carlos Alberto. Carlos Alberto was about as close to the kind of right back you see in the Premiership like Lee Dixon or Gary Neville as I was to Pele. One tactic was that the right-sided forward, Jairzinho, would cut in from the right. Since Italy played a man-marking defence, when Jairzinho did this the Italian left back, Facchetti, would go with him. This would in turn leave a huge gap down the right for Carlos Alberto to attack (figure 49). So he played the game like a winger, and when both he and Gerson joined the attack they were playing six up front. It was incredible to watch. On paper it was a 4–2–4 formation that Brazil played, but in reality you could describe it as 3–2–5 or even 3–1–6.

Carlos Alberto got so much of the ball in the 1970 final it was untrue. Bombing down the right he was the source of much of their play, and he popped up in the box to score Brazil's best goal, the last, which is one of the greatest goals ever scored. After a spell of passing lasting over a minute and including about thirty passes, the ball came to Pele just inside the box. With two men ahead of him his route to goal was blocked so he waited and waited before rolling the ball to

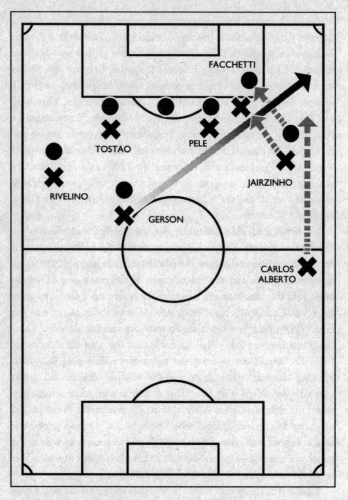

Figure 49: By drawing Italian left back Facchetti inside, Jairzinho's movement created acres of space for Brazil's attacking right back Carlos Alberto to exploit

his right just as television viewers around the globe saw Carlos Alberto charging into the picture. The Brazilian skipper came outside Pele at a terrific pace and struck the ball first time, low and hard into the corner.

Moments of brilliance in the match like this make it hard to talk about this team within the confines of a system because they were eleven sensational players. They did have a system, positions and a gameplan, but they took more risks than any team before or since. In fact, the only team which has ever come close to playing this way since, at international level, is the current Brazilian side coached by none other than Mario Zagallo – the coach in 1970.

During *Le Tournoi de France* in the summer of 1997 they took incredible risks. When they drew 3–3 with Italy they just poured forward. They got caught on the break several times but they seemed to accept that that might happen. I remember Ron Atkinson saying that it was the first time he had ever seen a team playing with a 'flat back one'. Of course that's not true, and the current side, just like the 1970 team, still have a set pattern that they must all slot into when they lose the ball.

It wasn't all natural talent and flair in Mexico in 1970. The players still had to work hard and earn the right to show off their skills. No team can rely on skill alone, not even one with the likes of Pele, Gerson, Rivelino and Jairzinho. There are times when tracking back, covering and hassling and harrying are as important as passing and shooting. That's why the central midfielder Clodoaldo was so important. He was Brazil's David Batty, if you like. Clodoaldo played the role that Nobby Stiles had played for England four years earlier. He protected what little defence the Brazilians had, broke up the play and gave the ball to the other midfield players to do the damage.

Brazil's back four in 1970 were nowhere near as good, as a defensive unit, as the England four in 1966 or, indeed, 1970. But solid defence wasn't part of the Brazilian gameplan. But the reliance on the men up front to score more goals than the defence conceded could have backfired on them because Italy had a lot of chances early in the match.

One thing that was particularly noticeable about the 1970 Brazil side, something you will also see in the modern Brazil side, is that they were not frightened to push two full backs forward at the same time. The left back, Everaldo, tended to be more defensive than Carlos Alberto on the right but they were never afraid to go tearing forward at the same time, leaving just two at the back.

Brazil played with the same outrageous disregard for defence in the 1982 World Cup, and this time they got caught out. They were 1–2 down to Italy with just a few minutes to go when all they needed was a draw to go through to the semi-finals, they kept pouring forward and eventually lost the game 3–2.

They really are a fascinating football nation, Brazil. They have gone through spells after 1970 – in 1974 and 1978 and, to an extent, 1990 and even 1994 when they won – when they thought they would make themselves a harder side. They tried to play a more European game with big, strong defenders and workmanlike midfielders but it didn't really work for them, and their fans hated it. But the way they played in 1970, and indeed the way they play now, is the way that they are expected to play. Attack at all costs and hang the expense. In the modern game Brazil are the only team who would even consider attempting such tactics, but then that's what they are all about. They've not really attempted all-out attack in the World Cup since 1970, except perhaps in 1982, because, I think, they did not believe they could do it again. They thought that the game had evolved too far in terms of other teams' defensive organisation, so they went for big centre forwards and hard men at the back and virtually played for 1–0 wins. It's only since they won the World Cup again in 1994 that they've gone back to the old beliefs, for despite their victory the team which won in the USA was widely criticised back home in Brazil for being dull to watch.

If they do play with this philosophy of out and out attack in the World Cup in France then it will be a bold decision, and will also make for some hugely entertaining football. They certainly have attacking talent to rival the 1970 side with players like Ronaldo, Romario, Denilson, Edmundo and Juninho plus incredibly adventurous full backs like Roberto Carlos and Cafu. But to play this system the coach has to believe that the two or three outfield players he leaves back in defence as the rest of the team charges forward can hold up the play for long enough when the ball is lost to allow two or three more to get back. If you are a defender in this situation and you are one on one with a forward, you don't tackle the attacker with the ball. You hold them up. If you can do that for five seconds then somebody can run forty yards and get back and help. I think that Brazil believe that although they might not be the best defenders in the world, if they can stay on their feet they can usually do enough to prevent a goal.

The one thing that might work against them is that when they play knockout football, chances are that in one game en route to the final or in the final itself they are going to come up against a side who will be able to stop them defensively and catch them on the break. Top international sides know that when they play Brazil the South Americans are going to create chances, but they know that they will give chances as well.

And that's why Brazil can be beaten. They commit so many men forward that, if you're good enough to hold them and then break quickly, you have a chance. Like most teams, when they get all their players back they are difficult to break down. You don't need great defenders if the midfielders are back and all the holes are filled. Nowadays that's even more the case because you don't get many tackles flying about in the midfield area – referees simply won't allow it. It's all about getting your body in the way and making people pass the ball around you, and you just pinch the ball when someone makes a mistake.

In many ways the legend of the 1970 World Cup Final is a long way from the reality of what actually happened. Everyone thinks Brazil wiped the floor with the Italians but, in fact, the Italians were well in the game until the later stages and at times they put Brazil under immense pressure on the counter-attack. The Brazilian defence always looked vulnerable. In the end, however, Brazil's total belief in their attacking play and their ability to score more goals than the other team was justified.

CHAPTER 10
Five at the Back

• •

Five at the back is something we had seen very little of in this country up until three or four years ago. Since the 1960s nearly every team in England had religiously played with a flat back four; it was the British way. Then, a couple of seasons ago, playing with three centre backs and two so-called wing backs suddenly became the thing to do. Teams like Liverpool, Chelsea and Aston Villa unveiled their new-look defences and it wasn't long before Sunday League managers up and down the country began experimenting with similar tactics.

Playing five at the back was seen as part of the growing influence of continental football in the Premiership, but the system which developed in English football was very different to the traditional sweeper system commonly played in Europe and South America. The system which has developed in English football gives you three central defenders who are permanently lined up in front of their own penalty area. It has evolved from the continental 'sweeper system' where you have two man markers – two centre backs who follow the opposition's two strikers wherever they go – plus a third centre back who is normally a good user of the ball.

This third player, the 'sweeper', drops behind the other centre backs to mop up anything that gets past them when the team is under pressure (figure 50), but when his team has the ball he steps out of defence to join in with the play. In the 1960s and 1970s Franz Beckenbauer was the master of this position for Bayern Munich and West Germany. A truly magnificent defender when faced with danger but then a majestic and graceful player who could hurt teams when

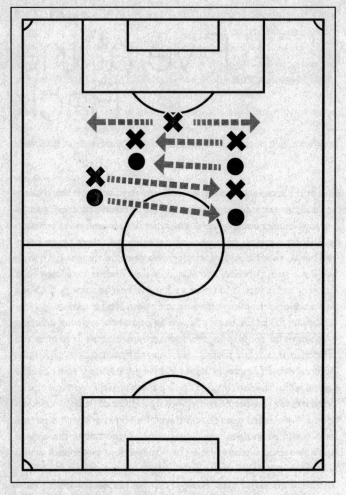

Figure 50: The continental 'sweeper' system with two man-marking centre backs and a deep-lying sweeper

he was in possession of the ball, *Der Kaiser* – as he was known – was the king of all sweepers.

Playing with a sweeper essentially means that you are playing with a spare man. Beckenbauer would adopt a position, at times twenty yards deeper than the last defender, and 'sweep' up whenever the ball came through to him. If any balls came over the top of the defence or anyone made a run through the defence, he would be there to pick them up. When you have the right player the sweeper will get the ball and bring it straight out of defence, joining the play and creating from deep.

The difference between this system and the one which has emerged in Britain in recent years – particularly in the Premiership – lies in the roles of the three central defenders. Unlike in the sweeper system, our centre backs mark zonally. What we are seeing is a defence which consists of a left-sided centre back, a middle centre back and a right-sided centre back. They stay in a line and pick up the opposition strikers as they come into their particular area of the pitch. There is no criss-crossing of defenders as there is with man marking when each defender follows his designated player wherever he goes (figure 51).

Think of Sol Cambell, Tony Adams and Gareth Southgate playing for England. They are always in a tight line, working as a unit and hardly ever switching positions. It's an extremely solid central defence. In an ideal world you would want a left-footed left centre back and a right-footed right centre back with the guy in the middle decent on the ball.

When you play this system the one thing you really need is mobile wide centre backs. Since the wing backs go forward, there's an awful lot of space between the wide centre backs and the touchline. So if forwards or midfielders spin into this area, you need your wide centre back to be able to get across and cover the danger (figure 52). That's why Glenn Hoddle played Tony Adams as the central centre back with the quicker, more mobile Sol Campbell and Gareth Southgate alongside him in the crucial World Cup qualifier against Italy in Rome in October 1997. The idea was that Campbell and Southgate could zip across to cover the flanks should an Italian get past one of the England wing backs. Against a side with a lesser attacking force Southgate would have played in the centre as the player who likes the

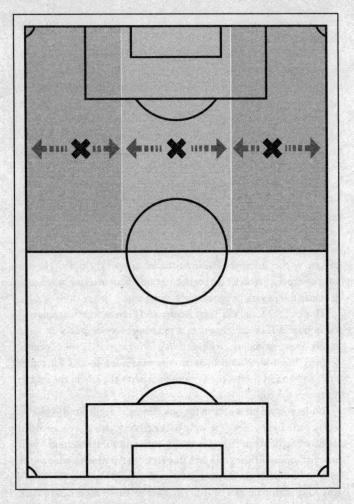

Figure 51: The 'British' system of three zonally marking centre backs

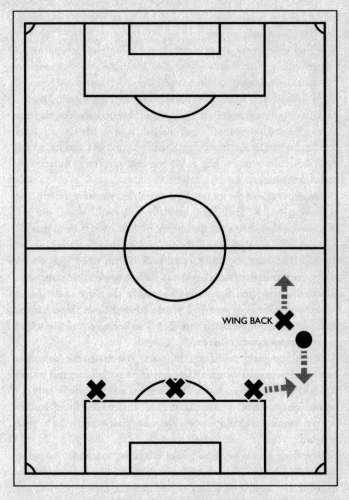

Figure 52: Because the right wing back has gone forward, the right-sided centre back must be quick and mobile enough to get across and cut out danger on the flank

ball at his feet most of the three and Adams would have played on one side of him as a stopper.

If you were to ask me to name three English players who would be perfect in a back three I would say Martin Keown of Arsenal on the right, Sol Campbell on the left and Dominic Matteo of Liverpool in the middle. You could see those three performing the three centre-back roles quite comfortably. They are all decent defenders, they are all mobile and they can all head the ball, and in Matteo you have someone who can link the defence with the midfield and the attack by coming out with the ball at his feet and spraying accurate long balls up the park.

On either side of the three central defenders, you have the left- and right-wing backs. They are essentially full backs when you are defending – they drop onto the outside of your back three to make it a line of five – but they have licence to go forward when you have got the ball. The thing about five at the back is that, when your goal is not under threat, both wing backs can push forward at the same time, effectively giving you five in midfield, while the three centre backs hold their positions. It's a 5–3–2 system when the other team has the ball, converting immediately into 3–5–2 as soon as you win it and begin to press forward (figure 53).

When the wing backs are in place you have five defenders protecting your goal. When all five defenders are lined up this system is very difficult to break down. One problem is that if you've only got two strikers to mark, or even just the one, then having five defenders is a bit excessive. But that's when you want your wing backs to push forward.

The wing back's job is to patrol the entire touchline. But when their team gets the ball neither wing back has to drop into the defence as cover. Unlike in a back four system they can both bomb forward at the same time, giving you two wide men high up the pitch at any one time. The problem here is that they can become relatively isolated. As they are the only wide men in the team they don't have anyone in front of or behind them to link with, whereas they would have a full back or wide midfielder in a 4–4–2 system. But what this system does give you is the possibility of getting the ball into good positions with

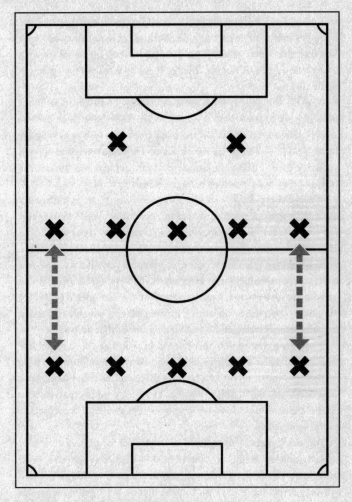

Figure 53: 5–3–2 becomes 3–5–2 when the wing backs push forward

both wing backs high up the field in positions to do damage. Imagine if you get into trouble on one side of the pitch, you can switch it to the other side where you will have a man waiting on the other wing in plenty of space. It doesn't involve the whole team shifting across (figure 54).

To make this system work the wing backs – I hate the name but it looks like we're stuck with it – are crucial. They have to be athletic enough to work up and down the pitch from box to box as they are the only wide players in the whole team. They must be good enough creatively to be effective in attack from an isolated position on the wing and they must be strong enough defensively to play as a full back.

If you are playing five at the back you have to think differently about the way your midfield shapes up. Normally people would go in with three central midfielders, with the idea being that your wing backs provide the width when you've got the ball and the wide protection when you haven't. If you are going to play this way you want players in the centre of midfield who can pass the ball and go forward. If you are going to give yourself a numerical advantage in midfield (when the wing backs are pushed up) then you want players capable of passing the ball through the midfield and making use of that advantage.

If you are going to play this system, I think that you do need one holding midfielder – someone like David Batty or Paul Ince – to hold the ball and break up attacks because there will be times when your wing backs are caught going forward. You then need two players who can be creative, unlock your opponents' defence and, most importantly, score goals.

You need goals from midfield because your wing backs are very rarely going to score. If you play 4–4–2 then your two wide midfielders should get you goals, maybe ten each a season, but you will very rarely see a wing back at the highest level getting ten goals a season. He can't commit himself to all-out attack in the same way as a wide midfield player because there is no cover behind him. So if you are going to deny yourself twenty goals a season from wide areas, you need the central midfield players to make up for the loss.

Aston Villa had a lot of problems at the beginning of the 1997/98 season – they lost their first four games – partly because they weren't

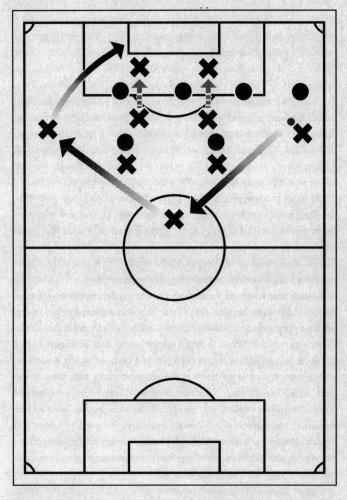

Figure 54: With two wing backs pushed forward a team can have width on both sides of the pitch at the same time

getting goals from midfield. Villa have played five at the back for a while now and if you look at the statistics they don't really get any goals from the wing backs, so they rely on their midfielders to get forward and score. People like Mark Draper, Ian Taylor and Simon Grayson must get into the box and score goals. The front two can't do it all. And at the start of the season the goals just weren't going in and Villa were all over the place. It was only when Draper and, in particular, Taylor started scoring that Villa's season began to take off. But I think they still need one other creative midfielder to get this system working successfully. They are very good defensively but the whole system grinds to a halt when their midfielders aren't on form.

Most of the wing backs who play, or have played, this system in the Premiership are more winger than full back. The players who play in the position in this country aren't great defenders. People like Jason McAteer, Graeme Le Saux, Dan Petrescu, Alan Wright and Fernando Nelson aren't brilliant defenders. I believe this fact is crucial to understanding why teams started playing this system.

I think that many of the managers who experimented with five at the back did it not because they thought it was a great formation but because they weren't confident in the ability of their defenders. Take Newcastle United. When Kenny Dalglish arrived at St James' Park I think he began playing five at the back not because of any great love of the system – after all he won the championship with four at the back at Liverpool and Blackburn Rovers – but because he wasn't confident of the defending ability of his full backs, people like Beresford and Barton, or his central defenders, people like Albert and Peacock, so he put an extra defender in there to try and tighten things up. And it worked. Newcastle may have stopped scoring goals for fun but they stopped letting them in as well.

Under Brian Little Aston Villa were one of the few sides that stuck with five at the back. However, on the opening day of the 1997/98 season, they went to Leicester and played four at the back. He wanted to accommodate three front men – Yorke, Collymore and Milosevic – instead of two, so he had to get rid of a defender. But it meant that they were very vulnerable out wide and particularly to crosses because their two full backs are not the best defensively. In a back four full backs must come into the box to defend crosses coming in from the opposite side, but Wright and Nelson simply aren't big and strong enough to battle in the air. Villa lost 1–0 that day to a back-post header from Marshall.

Little then went straight back to the system he'd been using for a couple of seasons – namely five at the back. The three centre backs could cover the entire width of the six-yard box and Brian expected them and his goalkeeper to deal with ninety per cent of crosses so the full backs rarely had to get involved.

In Wright and Nelson, and also Gary Charles, Villa have full backs who are pretty good going forward but are not so good defensively and this system accommodates them best. With five at the back they can bomb forward into midfield, both at the same time, while Villa still have the security of three centre backs. It will be interesting to see what John Gregory's long-term strategy will be.

No one has tried to play a traditional sweeper system in the Premiership because we simply do not produce the kind of players required. I don't just mean a sweeper but his support players as well – the man markers. Often I used to go off the pitch after a European game, down the tunnel and into the dresing room and wonder where my marker was, surprised he wasn't sitting beside me. Man-marking defenders stick to their strikers like glue and spend the whole game trying to stop them getting a kick. But because we have no history of playing like that, because I don't think it's part of the British mentality to play that way, we simply don't produce the right players. The closest is someone like Martin Keown of Arsenal who is probably England's best man marker, but Martin likes to get the ball on the ground and play a bit too.

On top of that we do not have an ideal sweeper. I think Glenn Hoddle would love to have a player like this within his three-man central defence. He wants a player who can step up into midfield when needed, but not an out-and-out sweeper. Hoddle was apparently thinking about using Jamie Redknapp of Liverpool in this role in *Le Tournoi de France* but he got injured. However, you can see Hoddle's thinking – Redknapp is good on the ball and has a great passing range.

I think it's strange that in a year when most club and international managers have reverted from five at the back to four, Glenn has persisted with five. It's what he believes in and obviously it's what he liked as a player, but it will be interesting to see if he ever changes his philosophy. There's no doubt that he wants a player who can play it out from the back and if he gets that then it will be quite different from the system that we've generally seen where the three centre backs have been relatively static. I believe he'd like to get closer to the continental system with two man-marking centre backs and a sweeper. I think that system is four or five years down the road for England, because we simply don't have a player who has been brought up to play as a sweeper. To get someone to play this position against the top international sides – the Italys, the Germanys and the Brazils of this world – would take a while. Rio Ferdinand or Jamie Redknapp might be able to do it against Zimbabwe, Zaïre or Morocco but that's totally different to doing it against the top sides.

Personally I wouldn't play five at the back if I were a manager, simply because I think it's an easier system to defend against. It's easier because the chances are more likely to come from central areas, where this formation is strong. It's very hard for the wing backs to get into really dangerous positions if they're up against a wide midfielder and a full back. I think it is very hard for wing backs both to create and score goals. They are the only wide players which means it is easier to isolate them, both in attack and defence.

I simply don't think that the pitch is big enough to need five players strung across it any more. When you have five at the back you have too many cooks spoiling the broth. In the modern game you will rarely find more than two forwards up against you. Sometimes you only have one. So if you play five at the back you've effectively got five players marking only one or two opponents. Players are so quick now that they can cover more ground than ever, so you shouldn't need to commit so many players to defence. In my opinion five gives you fewer options than four. With four at the back all your players are working together in little groups. Ultimately the only time I would ever play five would be if I really didn't think my defenders were good enough and I felt I needed to put an extra one in there to keep the other team out.

CHAPTER 11
Tactics for Europe

Compared to league football, embarking on a club campaign in Europe is like competing in a whole new ball game. Passionate and intimidating crowds, differences in style and tempo and even completely unfamiliar climates are the norm.

For a manager and his team European football presents a whole new set of technical, physical and tactical problems against which to pit their wits. During my playing career I used to relish these contests and, with Everton, I was lucky enough to win the European Cup Winners' Cup in 1985. European nights at Goodison Park were special nights charged with energy and passion, nights on which the eleven men in blue shirts truly felt that we carried the hopes of an entire nation on our shoulders.

Our manager, Howard Kendall, was someone who didn't spend a lot of time on the training ground working on methods or systems. We turned up, we played and we were usually the best team. The only time that Howard changed or tinkered with the tried and tested 4–4–2 system was in Europe. I always remember going to the Olympic Stadium in Germany to play Bayern Munich, who were probably the best team in Europe at the time, in the quarter-final of the 1985 European Cup Winners' Cup. I had a slight injury at the time which I think helped Howard because he wanted to make a change anyway for the away leg. He realised that the Germans had great strength in midfield. They had great footballers and he felt that the back four needed some extra protection. So he went with just Graeme Sharp up front on his own and brought Alan Harper into midfield and we played five across the middle (figures 55a and b).

We played a 4–5–1 system that night and the lads worked their socks off. They did a brilliant job. We hardly had an attack ourselves but the five midfielders protected the back four and denied the Germans the space they wanted by pressing and hustling. The lads denied the runners any room, stopped them from passing the ball and filled the midfield with bodies. It worked brilliantly and we drew 0–0 which was exactly what we wanted. It was a great result.

Then when we went back to Goodison we went back to 4–4–2, I came back into the side and we absolutely pulverised them. They hadn't seen me play before and they just couldn't cope with our power and pace, and we won 3–1.

The performance in the first leg had been down to our stifling tactics, but the second leg was down to pure power. We were 1–0 down at half-time in one of the biggest matches any of us had ever played but when Howard came into the dressing room all he said was: 'You're playing well. But they're frightened to death of Sharpey and Andy, they're frightened to death in the air, so I just want you to get it down and I want you to get it forward. Just knock it forward into Andy and Sharpey, get after it, and put them under pressure.'

Now that wasn't exactly a subtle tactic, but Howard had realised that they were frightened of our aerial power. He said: 'There's no point in passing it around, forget about that. When you get it, stick it in the box. From anywhere. Because they're petrified of Andy and Sharpey. Something will drop for us.' And that's exactly what happened. We banged in a couple of long throws, caused a bit of panic and before we knew it we were 2–1 up. Then we started passing it around, and the third goal was a classic.

The German manager came up to me in the tunnel after the game when I was about to be interviewed for television by Elton Welsby. I thought he was coming up to me to say, 'Well done, good luck in the next round,' but he just started jumping up and down, pointing his fingers and saying, 'You, you are a crazy man'. The player who had been man marking me had had his nose broken in two places but can you really believe that had anything to do with me?

It goes without saying that your approach to home and away

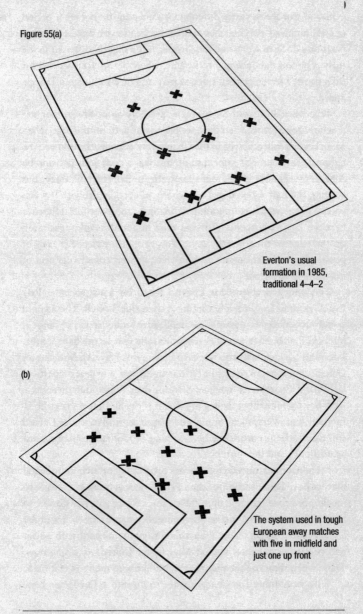

Figure 55(a)

Everton's usual
formation in 1985,
traditional 4–4–2

(b)

The system used in tough
European away matches
with five in midfield and
just one up front

games in Europe is vastly different. A European tie is over a period of 180 minutes – two matches of 90 minutes – so you have a different basis on which to work out your strategy. It's slightly different in the early stages of the Champions' League, where points are awarded for each game, but the general rules of playing home or away in Europe apply.

When British teams, for instance, are playing at home, they are much more effective when they are playing at pace. In the past, when Manchester United played in the Champions' League, they slowed the tempo of their natural game. I think this was a conscious decision by Alex Ferguson. He didn't want his team to give the ball away. But keeping the ball is one thing, it's what you actually do with it when you've got it which is important. Obviously there's a big difference between having possession in your own half and having possession on the edge of their penalty area. You can have eighty per cent of possession, but that doesn't do you much good if seventy per cent of it is in your own half.

This was a problem that Liverpool had for a while under Roy Evans, not just in Europe but in the Premiership as well. They would spend two minutes passing the ball across the back five and in midfield, but often it would never get anywhere near the danger area. I don't think it suits British teams to play in this way. All Manchester United's great home results in Europe in the last few years – particularly their Champions' League victories over Porto and Juventus – have been achieved by playing at pace. It is the hardest thing to do in football – after all, if the game was played at walking pace I could still play today – but it's the hardest kind of football to play against as well.

I think the reason why people are always saying that continental players have better technique than British ones is because they get so much more time on the ball in their games. Their game is slower, so they look better. They make fewer mistakes because they are under less pressure. British teams always used to press forward with power and precision and that is what Manchester United are doing now. Then, when they lose the ball, they work like wild men to get it back.

Why would any British team want to go into a European game

playing at a pace that they were not used to? A pace that their opponents' play every week – slow and laborious – it makes no sense. I think that it is crucial to up the tempo of the whole game, in order to ask European opposition questions that they wouldn't be asked in a league game back home. Whenever United have gone into games against top sides like Porto and Juventus and put them under the cosh the opposition has been made to look exceedingly ordinary.

Away from home it's a slightly different story. There are some games when you know that you will have to defend in numbers and you will not be able to go at the opposition like you would at home. No one is daft enough to think that you can go to somewhere like the San Siro, play AC Milan and dominate the game. The way you should approach a game like this is to make sure you don't concede a goal in the first twenty mintues. You set out your stall and try to silence the crowd.

In the Champions' League United will get the back four back in position in the early stages of an away match, the midfield four back and even one of their strikers, Teddy Sheringham, will drop into midfield. This still leaves them with Andy Cole lurking, ready to latch onto a quick break, use his electric pace and pick up something if it comes his way, but that's the way they go into the game.

If, after twenty minutes they haven't conceded a goal, they will then start to be a bit more adventurous. They will start playing it through the midfield a little more and asking some questions of their own. United do this brilliantly. It's something that not a lot of teams can do – just flicking a switch and upping the pace – but such is the confidence and ability of this side that they are able to control games in this manner. It is vitally important in Europe not to concede an early goal away from home. It gets the crowd going and gives your opponents confidence. Keeping them out for the first twenty minutes or half an hour has exactly the opposite effect.

You can tell that Fergie has made a conscious decision to play this cautious approach in European away games because in a Premiership match you never see United sit back. The difference in their tactics for domestic home and away games is minimal, because of the faith they have in their ability to score goals in league games and win them outright.

When it comes to traditional two-legged matches, the initial approach to the tie depends very much on whether you are drawn home or away for the first game. You often don't know what you're up against, so if you are away for the first leg send the side out prepared to be slightly cautious. Even if you are playing a supposedly weak Scandinavian team, you really can't be sure exactly what you're up against. They can't be that bad if they've made it into Europe. You can adopt a cautious approach both mentally and tactically. You urge your players to be cautious, and you can back that up by playing five in midfield, for instance, or, if you are playing five at the back, you can instruct your wing backs only to go forward one at a time so that you always have a solid four in place in defence.

If I was a manager I would spend the first half an hour assessing exactly what we were up against. You never get the full picture from videos of your opponents or scouting reports, so until you see them playing against your team you don't know where they pose a threat to you or where they have weaknesses which you might be able to exploit. Only once you were sure that they weren't going to be too dangerous would you become more adventurous, or, of course, you might try and get a message onto the pitch to say, 'Hold on, this team is useful, let's just keep it really tight, let's not do anything silly.' You would say, 'If we pinch a goal we pinch a goal, but let's make sure we don't concede or if we do that they only get one.'

If we were at home for the first leg I would send my team out in a positive frame of mind, pumped up for it. I would always like my team to start at a very high tempo in the home game. I would say, 'Get the ball into their half, get in amongst their defence and ask questions early on. Have a shot early.' It doesn't matter if it goes miles over, it will get the crowd going, and that's important. I believe that at any level. If after ten minutes you haven't got the early break-through, then it will be time for a more considered approach. But I would always say 'start quickly'. It's not much of a risk doing this because you can be fairly certain that, just as you would do, the away team is going to sit right back at the start of the game because they desperately don't want to give anything away.

As a player, I was always aware when we played away from home in a European tie that I was playing a completely different kind of football. Mentally I had to get myself tuned into the fact that there would be long periods of the game when I would be very inactive; I wouldn't see the ball. Now if you're a front man who is used to getting involved in the action all the time, that's sometimes hard. You have to get used to the fact that if the ball comes up to you then it's extremely precious and to give your mates a break you've got to get hold of it and keep it. You've got to protect it and keep the ball for five seconds until somebody gets up to you – to give your lads a break from defending.

At times in big European games when we were under tremendous pressure I would be spending more time in my own penalty area, getting back for corners and free kicks and heading and kicking the ball away, than I would be in the box at the other end where I was used to playing. But I think once you've put that into perspective you think, 'Yeah, I'll sacrifice my normal game for tonight because I know that in two weeks' time in the home leg the majority of the play is going to be at the other end and I'm going to be enjoying an awful lot of the ball. And just in the way that I've been disciplined tonight, at home the back four can be disciplined and give us the platform to score the goals at the other end.' You've just got to accept that that's par for the course when you're a striker playing away in Europe.

Before a big European game at Everton we didn't really prepare any differently than we would for a domestic game. If we were going to play five in the midfield we would walk through it on the training pitch. We would put the team out and just walk around the pitch with the ball, discussing where we should be when the ball was in different areas. The assistant manager, Colin Harvey, would walk with us, showing us exactly where he wanted the defence to push up to and little things like that.

Sometimes we might play the reserves in a game in which they played in the formation we expected our opponents to use. The trouble with that is you're not going to learn much if you have your third-choice striker taking the place of someone like Ronaldo.

We did have some little tactics which we would always use in

Europe, however. For instance, most foreign teams in those days played with two man markers and a sweeper (many still do). Now when we played at home against this system the first thing we would do was try to put the sweeper under pressure. In his domestic game he would always have been left alone – teams would drop off to the halfway line when he had the ball to try and cut off his passes. But we would try to upset him by snapping at his heels. They never liked it, and, quite often, if you upset the sweeper you upset the balance of the whole side.

I have to say that I always quite liked playing against a sweeper. I used to go and stand right next to him whenever we had a set play, a free kick or a throw-in. Since I was invariably being man marked my marker would go with me, so there would be this almost comical situation where they would be marking me two against one. Now if two men were marking me, it meant that somewhere on the pitch we had a spare man. The sweeper would step up five yards and I would step up with him and so would my marker. I tried to mess them up in this way and you could see the confusion on their faces – they just didn't know what was going on.

Away from home, as ever, it was a different story. We would leave the sweeper well alone. We would all get back behind the ball when they had it at the back, whether we were playing four at the back and four in midfield or four at the back and five in midfield, because we knew they weren't going to score in their own half. So we would all drop off and leave the sweeper with the ball. He couldn't score from seventy yards so rather than run about trying to press the ball we would save energy and use it when we won the ball back.

It's a bit like basketball where you say, 'OK, have the ball there. We'll let you come so far before we start putting you under pressure.' Whereas in the home leg we would be on the front foot, squeezing thirty or forty yards further up the pitch as a starting position and working from there. With our fans roaring us on we would really put ourselves about and try to get the opposition to make mistakes ten yards outside their own box.

The European game is one that we have had to re-learn since the post-Heysel ban on English clubs was lifted in 1990. Without a doubt the ban took a long time to get over. You can't lose five years of competing in Europe and not suffer. A generation of footballers came up who never played in Europe at club level. But I think the good things that people admired about our football then are still there: the competitive spirit, the strength and determination. However, whatever tactics and collective qualities you might have the game is all about the ability of individual players. In the 1997/98 Champions' League I watched Sergi of Barcelona, a man many believe is the best left back in the world, get absolutely pulverised by the pace and skill of Newcastle's Keith Gillespie.

I've always banged the drum for British sides in Europe. I've always said that there isn't a lot wrong with our game and that we're not far away from becoming feared again. Our younger players are learning again how to play in Europe. And, frankly, I don't think European sides like playing against us because we have a way of playing which marries the ability to play and pass the ball with the ability to play at pace. It's a potentially lethal combination.

CHAPTER 12
Liverpool 1977

• •

LIVERPOOL 3 BORUSSIA MONCHENGLADBACH 1
25 May 1977 (European Cup Final)
Olympic Stadium, Rome. Attendance: 52,000

Liverpool: (4–4–2)

Clemence

Neal   Smith   Hughes   Jones

Callaghan   McDermott   Kennedy   Case

            Heighway   Keegan

Borussia Monchengladbach: Kneib, Vogts, Klinkhammer, Wittkamp, Schaffer, Wohlers, Wimmer, Stielike, Bonhof, Simonsen, Heynckes

With the Kop recreated on the terraces of the Oympic Stadium, Liverpool were roared on from the start against the German champions in their bid to win the European Cup for the first time. The match didn't really come alive until the twenty-ninth minute when Terry McDermott raced into the area to latch onto a through ball and slip the Reds into the lead. After that everything seemed to be going to plan for the favourites and their star player, Kevin Keegan, who was playing his last game for Liverpool. But in the fiftieth minute, Liverpool were dispossessed on the edge of their own box and Danish star Alan Simonsen – who would one day play for Charlton Athletic

– put the Germans level. Suddenly Monchengladbach found their form and Ray Clemence was called into action to keep the scores level. Slowly but surely, however, Liverpool got their grip back on the game, passing neatly and controlling the tempo, and with twenty-three minutes to go they forced a corner. Steve Heighway fired the ball in and veteran defender Tommy Smith thundered a header in at the near post: 2–1. Now Liverpool had their tails up, they began turning on the style, and in the eighty-third minute Keegan broke through for what would have been the perfect send-off until he was crudely chopped down by Berti Vogts. Phil Neal slotted the penalty home, and Liverpool had done it. And as Liverpool fans have been saying ever since, 'when in Rome go absolutely crazy'.

When Liverpool won the European Cup in 1977, becoming only the second English club to do so after Manchester United's triumph in 1968, it was the culmination of thirteen consecutive years of European competition. And after that first triumph, achieved in the splendid setting of Rome's Olympic Stadium, they went on to become the dominant force in European football for the next eight years.

Playing their own very distinctive brand of 4–4–2, the Merseyside giants won the cup again in 1978, 1981 and 1984. Their very name sent shudders of fear down the spines of continental opponents. At home it was a similar story, and under Bob Paisley and later Kenny Dalglish they were an almost invincible force in the league, winning ten titles in the fifteen years between 1975 and 1990.

In those days Liverpool had great players in every department, but for me the real secret of their success was the defence. They played with a back four, but it was a back four with a difference. The key players were the centre backs. Every Liverpool team I ever played against had a pair of centre backs who were not the kind of players that I would play against in any other game of the season. They weren't the traditional towering giants whose only job was to win everything in the air and welly the ball out of danger. Liverpool's centre halves were always stylish footballers.

They had people like Phil Thompson and Emlyn Hughes, Alan Hansen and Mark Lawrenson. You wouldn't call any of those players classic centre halves. They were good in the air, they could tackle and get stuck in, but they could also use the ball when they had it at their feet. They were skilful and composed on the ball in the tightest of situations.

When I was playing we would decide which of the opposition's defenders to leave with the ball – the one least likely to hurt us. And we would invariably find someone at the back, usually a centre back, who we felt didn't have the passing ability to cause us any problems, and then we would go and mark all the other players so that he would have to play it long. But when we played against Liverpool we couldn't leave any of them with the ball because they were all so good.

Consequently, the play nearly always started at the back with Liverpool. They had players able to build up from the back, to keep possession, to probe and wait for a chance to pounce. They always seemed to be in control. It's not uncommon to see this style of play in the Premiership now – teams like Chelsea, Manchester United and the current Liverpool side do it to great effect – but the Liverpool of the late 1970s and early 1980s probably did it better than any English club side before or since.

When the right back – in the 1977 European Cup Final against Borussia Monchengladbach it was Phil Neal – had the ball but his route forward was blocked, he would be quite happy to come inside and stroke it inside to his centre back. In Europe, particularly, it was crucial to keep the ball because when you lost it you knew the continental sides, with their excellent technique, wouldn't give it back easily. In an awful lot of English teams, both then and now, if the right back can't go forward he just plays a hopeful ball down the line, giving the opposition a good chance of nicking in and winning the ball or simply breaking down the attack. But Liverpool had this incredible patience.

When they played this way it meant that the team they were playing against could never line up their midfield and defence as they would have liked. They were never set. Teams would try to make the right back play the ball down the right. They would flood players into the right-hand side of the pitch and then pressure the ball, forcing him to play a long ball right into the area of the pitch where all their players were waiting (figure 56). But Liverpool would counter this by quickly transferring the ball from right to left and suddenly they would be attacking over on the left where their opposition was weakest (figure 57).

So when the route ahead of him was blocked Phil Neal would turn inside and play a square ball across the pitch to Phil Thompson who would be standing level with him. Thompson would take one touch and feed Emlyn Hughes on his left and Hughes would quickly pass it on to the left back Joey Jones on the opposite touchline. In the space of a few seconds the ball had crossed the pitch and Liverpool were attacking the side where all the space was. And space, of course, is the most valuable commodity in a football match.

By the time the opposition midfielders and defenders had come across to the left-hand side, in the space of four passes Liverpool had advanced twenty yards up the pitch into the danger area and the full back had the ball in an area where he could influence the play. If Neal had just pumped it forward instead of passing inside to his centre back it would have been a fifty/fifty ball and a good chance for the defence to either gain possession or clear the danger.

This ability to pass the ball was spread throughout the Liverpool team, but it was so unusual for a pair of centre backs to be so capable. When I played against them for Aston Villa and Everton there were long spells when we simply couldn't get the ball. Normally you count how many chances you get in a game, but I used to count how many kicks I got at Anfield, such was their domination. It's a lot harder physically when you don't have the ball because all you are doing is running up and down while they just stroke the ball to one another. Liverpool didn't often go into games and have long spells when they didn't have the ball.

In the 1977 European Cup Final they had a midfield of Jimmy Case on the right, Ian Callaghan and Terry McDermott in the centre and Ray Kennedy on the left. They were all masters of the ball but tireless workers at the same time. In many ways this group played similarly to England's 1966 World Cup side in that the midfielders often switched positions to confuse their opponents.

It was a pretty classic 4–4–2 midfield. It had two wide men but

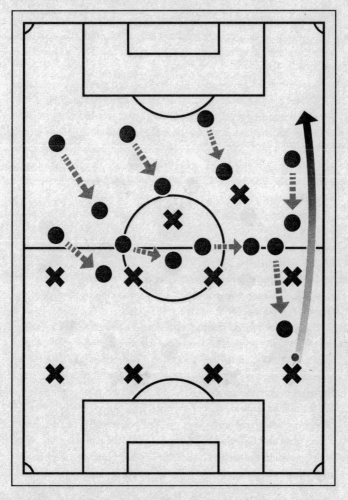

Figure 56: The team which doesn't have the ball closes down the right-hand side of the pitch, drawing the right back into a speculative ball down the line

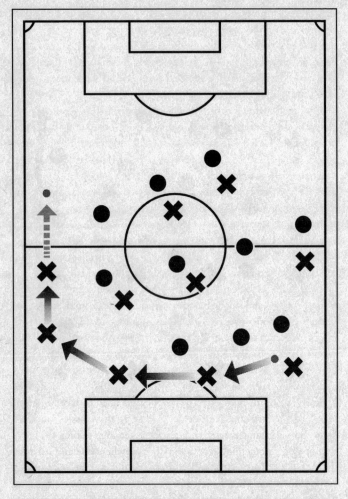

Figure 57: In this situation, Liverpool would play the ball across the back and open up the less heavily congested left flank

they weren't traditional wingers by any stretch of the imagination. Jimmy Case on the right epitomised the qualities you need as a wide midfield player. He had the ability to get forward and influence the game in the attacking third, but he also had the ability to get back and cover for Phil Neal when they lost it. And Case never really wandered too far from that right-hand side.

On the left-hand side it was slightly different. Ray Kennedy was certainly not a winger. He was naturally left footed and took up a position on that left-hand side, but his job was to get into the box, attack and score goals. Having been a highly successful striker at Arsenal before switching to Anfield he certainly had the ability to do that. He was particularly dangerous when the ball was coming down the right. Imagine you are Phil Neal or Jimmy Case coming down the right, and you know that if you angle a ball over the centre backs to the far post Ray Kennedy is going to be there. That's a great outlet to have. He would always be there and he was brilliant in the air, certainly better than most of the full backs who marked him.

Neal and Case got to the stage where they could angle in a ball from the right-hand side without even having to look up. If they were struggling or under pressure they knew that they could serve the ball in and nine times out of ten Ray would be there. And usually he would win it. And I don't think the full back would fancy too much looking over his shoulder and seeing Ray Kennedy bearing down on him, attacking the ball.

In the centre of midfield Liverpool always liked to have a player who got forward and Terry McDermott is the classic example. Sometimes if a game is tight and the front men aren't doing the business you need something to come from somewhere else and running from deep was Terry McDermott's forte. He did it as well as any and better than most. Then they had a playmaker. They always liked to have someone behind with a bit of steel, someone who could win the ball, put their foot on it to calm things down and then use it intelligently. In this game it was Ian Callaghan, a classic central midfield Liverpool player. He was good on the ball, but with the grit and determination to compete for every ball as if his life depended on it.

In central midfield, rather than playing the two players side by side they liked to get one ahead of the other. One sitting, holding and spraying the passes about and the other going forward, getting into the box from deep areas and attacking the ball. It's not that the players were restricted to these duties, there was plenty of scope for the holding player to bomb forward while the other held back, but in this team, for example, you knew that McDermott was going to go forward as much as possible. You knew that he was the runner. But it was still interchangeable. If Callaghan spotted a space then McDermott would just hold his position.

Liverpool dominated the early stages of the match, controlling the game from the back and hunting the ball tigerishly whenever the Germans gained possession. With great sides like this Liverpool team people always remember the great goals, the great moves. But the right to be able to play that kind of football has to be earned. When this Liverpool side lost the ball they dropped back into position and hunted tigerishly to get it back. Players like Case, Souness and later McMahon were great ball players but they were hard as nails at the same time. The Liverpool side of the last few years, certainly before they signed Paul Ince, has lacked a similar player. They could pass the ball like Brazil but they didn't have the determination necessary to win it back and start all over again.

Another thing about Liverpool in this era was that, despite their domination of most games, they rarely overcommitted themselves. You very rarely saw both full backs forward at the same time. They went forward methodically, which meant they were hardly ever caught out at the back. They didn't really look to push up at the back either. They didn't look for offside because they didn't need to. They would defend quite deep inside their own half, far enough back so that they didn't leave a huge gap behind them for a nippy striker to exploit if the ball was played over the top. They had good enough defenders to deal with most situations so they didn't need to take the gamble of playing offside. When you play offside there is always the risk that you might get caught out.

Liverpool weren't really that interested in winning the ball if Borussia Monchengladbach had it deep in their own half. Instead, they dropped deep into their own half, got tight as a unit – two banks of four – and challenged the Germans to come up with something good enough to break them down. In this way they restricted the space in which their opponents had to play. They effectively made the pitch smaller so that, to get through, Monchengladbach would have to get past eleven players in an area which was basically the Liverpool half plus ten yards or so (figures 58 and 59).

Up front Liverpool had, for me, a classic front two. Usually it was Kevin Keegan and John Toshack but, because Toshack was dropped to the subs' bench for the Monchengladbach game, Steve Heighway played in his place. This was actually Keegan's last game for Liverpool since he was leaving to play for Hamburg in Germany the following season but he was simply magnificent in a red shirt. His movement was superb. He would buzz around Toshack and Toshack's ability to find him with flicks and little passes around the edge of the box was remarkable. I know from experience that you get to know where your partner is going to run, but the understanding comes from hard work on the training ground. Strikers will play together without opposition, getting players to feed ball after ball to them until they always know what the other will do in any given situation.

There is not a lot more that you can say about Liverpool tactically because, with the addition of ball-playing centre backs they played a fairly classic game. They were a classic team with three units – defence, midfield, attack – working independently but all clicking together at the same time. They had truly great players playing a simple system and they played it magnificently. Liverpool had had a successful system ever since Bill Shankly took over the reins in the 1950s and they stuck to it.

It's a cliché but no one player was ever bigger than the club. Shanks or Paisley would bring in promising young players and put them in the reserves for two years to learn the Liverpool way. Shankly once said, 'the best team after Liverpool is Liverpool reserves,' and it was probably true. When Tommy Smith was injured, in came Phil Thompson who played exactly like Tommy. When Tommy Smith and Phil Thompson were both out of the team, along came Alan Hansen and Mark Lawrenson to play exactly the same way.

They did have great players, but in my opinion they had ordinary

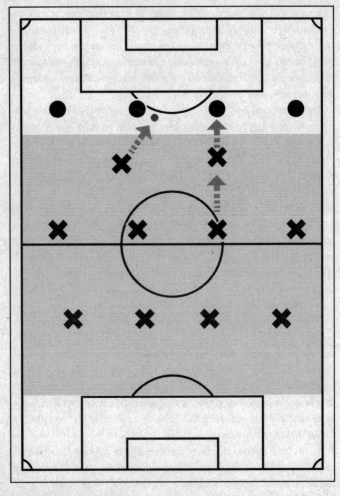

Figure 58: The spread of play in a typical English league game, with the strikers pushing right on to the opposition defence

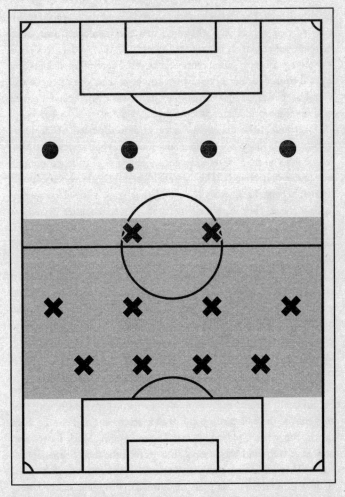

Figure 59: By dropping back into their own half, in Europe Liverpool restricted the space in which their opponents could play

players as well. But the system was so strong and the players' knowledge of that system was so strong, that they could get away with having weaker players in some positions. OK, they had a great spine – a good goalkeeper, good centre backs, good central midfielders and a good front two. But I think when you have that, you can get away with less quality on the outside. Joey Jones was a good player, but he was never a world beater at left back.

Liverpool also had a psychological grip over football. Anfield was a fortress. Having played there many times and had so few victories, let me tell you that the ones we got we enjoyed. But I loved running out under that famous 'This is Anfield' sign just above the players' tunnel, seeing the Kop sway behind that goal. I loved competing against them. They were the benchmark like Manchester United are now. A lot of teams would go there and be beaten before they even ran out onto the pitch. I think that Manchester United have that now at Old Trafford.

I went to Anfield with Villa in 1978, when they were European champions, and we were the first team to beat them there for eighteen months. I scored both goals. We just played well that day. We had as much of the ball as they did and we got lucky. We put them under as much pressure as they put us under and beat them 2–1. I scored one at each end, the winner in front of the Kop from a setpiece. What a moment.

To beat them you knew you had to match them. You needed to be physically strong and you needed to be fit because the way that they moved the ball meant you had to keep chasing and closing them down. But when I played against Tommy Smith, Mark Lawrenson and Alan Hansen, I was always anxious to ruffle their feathers physically. They loved time on the ball to stroke it about, but what I tried to do was put them under pressure. Instead of dropping off and letting them have the ball, which always happened in Europe, a good tactic was (in fact, I still think it's a good tactic against a passing team like Liverpool) to try to win the ball off the back four. When the ball was being played around at the back I would be right there, hassling Alan Hansen or Tommy Smith, putting them under pressure and trying to win the ball.

Liverpool didn't like to knock it up front aimlessly. Although Toshack was a big man people like Keegan and Dalglish didn't want the ball in the air. So I used to get whoever I was playing with up front to push up and take a chance. We would be pushing and tackling and making their central defenders play it when they didn't want to. Many teams were so frightened of Liverpool that they would back away and let the back four have the ball. When you did that against this Liverpool side they just kept passing the ball across the back four until they spotted a gap.

They were so used to getting time on the ball that when you closed them down you could see they were getting rattled. They were arrogant with the ball and quite rightly so, they were the best players in the land. But if you really got in there and roughed them up a bit their passing would become less accurate and that gave you a chance to influence the game. They got flustered as well. I remember I sent Phil Neal into the crowd once when he was just clearing a ball. I came across him and knocked him into the touchline making him fall across the track. He got up and started shouting at me and I just said, 'What? This is a man's game.'

The full backs were normally very, very confident when it came to picking the ball up from the goalkeeper. Very rarely did you see Clemence or Grobbelaar kick the ball out, they would nearly always try to roll it to a defender. But if you look at Steve Heighway and Kevin Keegan, not the biggest of men, any pair of half-decent centre backs would fancy their chances in the air against them. That's why when I looked at the 1977 European Cup Final again I couldn't understand why the coach of Monchengladbach didn't tell his forwards to push up when Clemence had the ball to prevent him throwing it out. It was never the continental way to defend from the front in this way, but it played into Liverpool's hands in Europe. It meant that they could control the game from the back.

Apart from when they were under pressure at the back, the only other area where you might say this Liverpool side had a weakness was in the air. When you looked at the centre backs like Tommy Smith and Emlyn Hughes they were never the biggest, they weren't six-foot plus and dominant in the air. They were good movers, quick on their feet, so you looked at where they might be a little bit weak and certainly I always fancied my chances against them aerially. I thought if we could get the ball in the box in good areas and good angles then I might get a good chance of scoring. That's an area where I always thought they could be exploited. The goal I scored in front of the Kop in 1978 was from a free kick. The ball came into the box where I muscled Joey Jones out of the way, got it down on my chest and smashed it in.

But that was just one match, and most of the time I played against them they ran us ragged. Against Monchengladbach, apart from conceding a sloppy equaliser after Phil Neal was caught out of position, Liverpool always looked in control. Again we can talk about the tactics they played, but you look at the team and you don't see a single player who isn't comfortable on the ball and capable of scoring a goal. If the quality of the players wasn't good enough they wouldn't have been such a force, whatever system they played.

CHAPTER 13
Underdog
Tactics

● ●

In a hundred-metre race it's pretty rare for the fastest sprinter to lose. At a major golf tournament it is invariably the best player over the four days who triumphs. In football, however, the better team often leaves the pitch with the bitter taste of defeat in its mouth. You can have the ball for eighty per cent of the game, you can hit the crossbar five times, but if the other team nicks a lucky goal and you don't score then when the final whistle blows you have lost. Unlike a boxing match, the result of a game of football is not determined by a panel of judges, you don't get marks for artistic interpretation, and that's why at the start of every match, every team, no matter how small, has a chance.

Just look at some of the great upsets in football history. Hereford beat Newcastle in 1972, Colchester beat Leeds in 1971, the USA beat England in 1950. There is always a chance for the underdog, and there are certain tactical ways of improving that chance quite dramatically.

What you can do with tactics is stifle a team. You can destroy, you can make life difficult. I've always said that it is easier to be destructive than to be constructive. That's why strikers cost £15 million and defenders don't. That's why it's easier to organise a tight defence than it is to plan a way through one. That's why the best players in the world are all front men or quality midfielders – because they have a talent to break down defences.

Take Leicester City's win in the Coca-Cola Cup Final last season. Martin O'Neill, the Leicester manager, looked at Middlesbrough, and realised that if he sent his team out to play their natural game they would be beaten. Boro's Brazilian international midfielder and by far and away their most influential player, Juninho, had already masterminded a crushing defeat on his side in a home game earlier in the season. So he decided to man mark Juninho.

He didn't change Leicester's system dramatically, but he played Pontus Kamaark and told him to do nothing in the game but mark Juninho. He instructed him to follow the Brazilian wherever he went and get so close to him that he wouldn't be able to exert an influence on the game. He knew that if Kamaark did his job then Juninho wouldn't see nearly as much of the ball as he usually did because no one would pass to a man with a marker standing right next to him. Even if he did get the ball he wouldn't have the space to play his normal game. What O'Neill was essentially doing was sacrificing one of his men to try and nullify their main threat, and then take his chances with a match which was effectively ten against ten.

Playing this way is a very big gamble, because if your man marker isn't up to the job, or the player he is marking is so good that he gets the better of him, you are effectively playing with a man short. Your man marker is going to be so obsessed with his stifling duties that you won't get much from him when you've got the ball. So you've got to have the right kind of player to the job. Man marking isn't easy, in fact it's a horrible job. If you don't get it right then you are in trouble.

Sometimes, however, you just need the rub of the green to get a result. I remember when Sheffield Wednesday went to Liverpool during the 1996/97 season and won 1–0. All Sunday I read about how this had been an incredible tactical victory for David Pleat, a manager who is very much into systems and tactics. I read how Peter Atherton had man marked Steve McManaman and that it had worked a treat. Now I watched that game and in all honesty Liverpool could have won 7–2. They hit the woodwork four times, Kevin Pressman made about half-a-dozen world class saves, and yet it went down as a great tactical victory. On another day, had half of those chances gone in, it might have been described as a tactical disaster. So talk of tactics and systems can sometimes cloud the issue. David Pleat got lucky. Most teams these days try to man mark McManaman and most of the time it doesn't work because he's too good. It didn't really work on this occasion because McManaman should have scored six that day. But he didn't and Pleaty was hailed a tactical genius. In fact, his goal-keeper won him that game.

You often get shocks, particularly in cup football, because teams set their stall out not to be beaten. Now if you set your stall out to do that then you might nick one at the other end against the run of play and win 1–0. People will say what a great tactical coup when really it was a hard-earned but slightly fortunate win.

I was 18 when I was involved in the first bit of tactics of my playing career, and it failed miserably. It was the 1974 Scottish Cup Final when I was playing for Dundee United against Celtic. Now Dundee United hadn't got into a cup final for years and years. Our manager, Jim McLean, normally a very positive man, felt that the centre back who I was going to play against, Billy McNeill – a Scottish interna-tional, a stalwart and a giant of a man in Scottish football – was too good for me. Even though I was scoring goals for fun at the time he thought he would try to come up with a tactical plan to overcome this problem.

So he played me on the left-hand side of the attack instead of right down the middle where I had been playing all season. The idea was to try and get the rest of the team to work the ball down the right whenever they could and then, when the ball came into the box, I would be able to attack it from out wide. Jim McLean felt if I was running into the box from deep I would have more chance of losing my marker and getting in a good header (because I would be taking a running jump rather than a standing one). That was the tactic. That was the ploy.

He told me this in the week before the game and I didn't agree with him. I was young enough and brash enough to say, 'I'll play against McNeill. I think I'm good enough to play against him.' And I think I was right. We made it easy for him. Our entire system relied on getting good crosses in from the right side but this didn't happen, and whenever the ball came down the left I was picking it up and trying to be a left winger. I was crossing the ball into the box where I should have been, and Celtic lapped it up with ease.

At half-time we were 2–0 down and Jim McLean abandoned the plan. I went back to playing in the middle and in the second half we were a different team. I'll never forget one moment when suddenly a cross came in from the left, I lost McNeill and I met the ball with my head from about seven yards. I headed it as firmly as I've ever headed a football in my life and was sure it was a goal. But the goalkeeper, Dennis Connaghan, made one of the best saves ever made against me. Somehow he got his fingertips to it and flicked it over the bar.

Had that gone in, the whole game would have been different because of the changes we had made at half-time. In the end Celtic got a late one and ended up winning 3–0 but there's no doubt we made a better fist of it in the second half. That was my first experience of tinkering with the system and it didn't work. Sometimes you've just got to believe in your own ability even if you are the underdogs, because the best chance you've got is playing your own game and hoping you get lucky.

There are, of course, no guarantees that what you try will work. If I was the Everton manager and we were playing Manchester United at Old Trafford tomorrow, I'm sure most people would tell me that I had to try something to stop them but the question is what? Who do you man mark? Giggs? What about Scholes? What about Beckham? What about Cole? What about Sheringham?

You can change little things, but the most important thing is to go out there and give everything you've got. If you are going to beat Manchester United then you are going to have to compete in midfield. I would almost go in man for man against them in that area, not just one marking the main playmaker, but four on four. I would instruct each member of my midfield to take responsibility for one of their midfielders. Stopping them is the key to stopping United.

I would never go in with five at the back because you could never allow Giggs the chance to go one on one against your right wing-back because he would skin him at some point. You need to have a midfielder tracking him all the time with your right back there as well so that he is forced to fire in hopeful crosses (figure 60). It would be the same with Beckham on the other side, although I would tell the player on Beckham to rough him up a bit, just to rattle him. I think

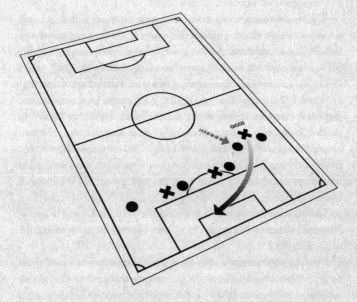

Figure 60: By double banking on Giggs you try to force him to play in hopeful crosses

if Beckham has a weakness it's his temperament and I think you can use that. Get players to wind him up a bit, and that can put him out of his stride. Then in the centre of midfield you would need two fit lads to stick with Scholes and Butt.

The trouble with going man for man in midfield is that at some point you've got to ask yourself the question, 'Where can we expose them?' And it's difficult. If United are vulnerable anywhere it's at the back. They do tend to hold their line quite high up the pitch and I think you can get in behind them. On top of that I don't think they are entirely happy with anything that goes across goal between the goalkeeper and the centre backs. I don't think there's any point in playing high balls at them because Johnsen and Pallister, the two centre backs, will deal with them easily. The only time I have seen them really troubled has been when their opponents have used good movement and pace up front with the ball played on the ground. Darren Huckerby of Coventry City had their defence all over the place by running at them with pace during the Premier League game at Highfield Road in December 1997 and City ended up winning the game 3–2.

I would play with two up front against United because you've got to give their defenders something to worry about. You need good, intelligent movement from your strikers and you would hope that they could carve out a chance at some time in the game. Your midfield and your defence would also need to have a good day.

If you look at the current Manchester United team their main goalscoring threat is the pace of Cole. I would therefore tell my defenders not to defend high up the pitch. There's no point in getting caught level with Andy Cole, you must always drop two yards off him so that he can't just turn you and get ahead of you in a race for the ball. But if he gets it in at his feet you are still between him and the goal and he's still got to do something pretty special. If he gets it in behind you high up the pitch you're in trouble.

I would tell my midfield and defence not to worry too much if United had the ball in deep, wide areas. I would tell them to get in front of Giggs and Beckham and make sure they don't advance any further. You don't want them getting to the by-line, but if they want to cross it in from deep, that's fine. That's because if there's one area where United aren't a huge threat from open play, it's in the air. If you've got them tossing in balls from forty yards away the centre backs should be able to beat Sheringham and Cole, who aren't that big or strong.

At the other end, attention to detail at setpieces is crucial. They may well be your only chances of nicking something from the game. You need to devise setpieces where you move people like Pallister and Johnsen, their best men in the air, out of position. You've got to test them. You also need to work on counter attacking, on trying to break quickly, because you know that you're going to be under pressure in the game and that, at times, Giggs, Beckham and Scholes will all push right forward. So when there is a break on you've really got to go for it and not just be grateful for a breather from defending. Once the United midfielders are back they are a very, very difficult team to break down.

I don't think there is any point in going to Old Trafford simply to defend because whatever you do, at some point United are likely to snatch a goal. You're much better off going there and giving them something to worry about at the back instead of sitting back and virtually admitting defeat, just hoping to escape without a drubbing. But a lot of managers go to Old Trafford these days not to get a win or even a draw, but to not get beaten 6–0.

Motivation for a game like this should not be a problem. If I had a bunch of players who I had to convince that they could get a result at Old Trafford then I would be getting a new set of players pretty sharpish. I wouldn't have a player in the side who didn't believe that we could get a result anywhere. It might be more difficult at Old Trafford but there's nothing to say it's impossible. Mind you, one other thing I would do in the week before the game is spend plenty of time praying.

The tactics I have talked about will only play a small part because games like this are all about being mentally strong. If you are the manager of a team of professional footballers who have made it to the Premiership then that shouldn't be a problem – this kind of game is the very reason that they are there. The players should want to be remembered as the team that went to Old Trafford and won. Part of being a good team is having the mental togetherness to overcome situations where the odds are stacked against you. If you've got that then the best way to get them prepared for the game is to take them to Old Trafford and let them hear the noise of the crowd.

As a manager it's your job to ensure that you have a group of players who believe in themselves and who believe in you. Respect is of the utmost importance. I hope I would have had respect from the players for what I had achieved as a player, but I would have had to earn their respect as a manager. I would never have asked any player to do something that I wouldn't have been prepared to do myself as a player. Then you have to get them to believe in the way you want them to play. The manager has his beliefs and, and after a couple of months, he will know which players are suited to the way he wants to play and which players believe in him. Those that don't believe will have to go – it's as simple as that – and others will have to come in. You know the way you want to play and if the players don't believe in it then they can go elsewhere. It doesn't matter who they are, it doesn't matter how much their departure will upset the fans, if a player isn't giving you everything he's got then you are better off without him.

Going out onto the pitch as an underdog can often be inspiration enough. Wimbledon, for instance, only ever seem to really struggle in matches when they are favourites to win. I'm sure that's all part of the 'the world is against us' atmosphere that Joe Kinnear creates in the dressing room. His team absolutely relishes going to the big clubs and upsetting the odds.

CHAPTER 14
Wimbledon 1988

● ●

WIMBLEDON 1 LIVERPOOL 0
14 May 1988 (FA Cup Final)
Wembley Stadium. Attendance: 98,203

Wimbledon: (4–4–2)

Beasant

Goodyear   Thorn   Young   Phelan

Cork   Sanchez   Jones   Wise

Fashanu   Gibson

Liverpool: Grobbelaar, Gillespie, Ablett, Nicol, Spackman, Hansen, Beardsley, Aldridge, Houghton, Barnes, McMahon

While the whole world tuned in to see the great Liverpool team which had just won the league destroy the rough and tumble upstarts from Plough Lane to claim 'the double', Wimbledon decided to change the script. The scene was set in the fourth minute when Vinnie Jones, sporting a particularly fetching new haircut, went thundering into a tackle with the Reds' own hard man Steve McMahon and sent him flying. Wimbledon weren't at Wembley for a nice day out. The game's major turning point came in the thirty-fifth minute when Liverpool's

Peter Beardsley got the better of the Wimbledon defender Andy Thorn, pulled clear and stuck the ball in the back of the net...only to discover referee Brian Hill had blown his whistle for a Liverpool free kick. John Barnes' kick went sailing over the bar and a minute later the Dons were ahead. Dennis Wise floated in a free kick on the edge of the Liverpool box and Lawrie Sanchez rose at the near post to flick it in at the far corner. Now Liverpool had a battle on their hands. The Reds huffed and puffed but the longer the game went on the less likely it looked that they would break down the resilient Wimbledon defence – until they were awarded a penalty for Clive Goodyear's 'trip' on John Aldridge. Aldridge himself took the kick, but Dave Beasant hurled himself to his left and straight into the history books as the first goalkeeper to save a penalty in a Wembley FA Cup Final. From then on there only ever looked like being one winner.

A lot of people had said that it would be a disaster for football if Wimbledon won. They hated this team which had no respect for footballing tradition and whose strength was not neat passing and moving but hoofing the ball up to a big centre forward and causing chaos in their opponents' penalty area. The so-called purists said that Liverpool had to win to preserve the future of football. However, I thought that it was fantastic that this tiny little club could come from nowhere and win the FA Cup. The idea of a bunch of players who were either cast-offs from other teams or plucked from non-league football turning up at Wembley and beating the best team in the land was so seductive. If Liverpool really were this great team, how could they be beaten by a bunch of hoofers and former hod carriers?

But the football that Wimbledon played was hardly the kind to get you drooling. It wasn't pretty to watch and in many ways this victory did set football in this country back. Wimbledon had a very basic but finely tuned and perfectly executed strategy, and for a while very few teams could cope with it. And I think that for a little while, a lot of the smaller clubs tried to copy them.

Long-ball football has its roots way back in the 1950s when, under legendary manager Stan Cullis, English First Division side Wolverhampton Wanderers won three championships and two FA Cups between 1954 and 1960. Wolves' strategy was to boot the ball forward whenever the opportunity arose and for the attackers to follow it up at full speed. Although it was highly successful, the system was fiercely criticised with observers saying it prevented players using their full range of skills. But Cullis didn't listen. He even used the 1953 Hungary v England game to defend his tactics. He defiantly announced that the Hungarians played ninety-four long passes at Wembley that day and that everyone still raved about how beautifully they had played.

But despite the silverware which graced the Molineux trophy cabinet in the 1950s, few teams went the Wolves way and it wasn't until Graham Taylor became manager of Watford in June 1977 that serious long-ball football resurfaced in England. Watford had just finished seventh in Division Four when Taylor took over, but by 1983 they were runners up to Liverpool in the First Division. Taylor opted for an out-and-out long-ball game although he did have players of quality – John Barnes being the obvious example – who could use it cleverly around the box.

Around the same time, Charles Hughes, the man seen as the guru of the long-ball game, was beavering away as the FA's Director of Coaching. Despite never having actually played professional football, Hughes was an advocate of direct (but not necessarily long-ball) football. Having scientifically analysed the game he came up with the astonishing fact that eighty-five per cent of goals are scored from a move involving five passes or less, which led him to reason that there was little point in possession football. 'When the right attitude is combined with high levels of fitness and technical expertise, the right method – direct play – truly becomes a winning formula,' argued Hughes in his book *The Winning Formula*.

Many managers and coaches were influenced by Taylor and Hughes and many teams experimented with the long-ball game. Watford continued to thrive after finishing runners-up in the league in 1983 and the following year reached the FA Cup Final. They were, however, beaten 2–0 at Wembley by some team called Everton and it's funny but the name of the bloke who scored the second goal escapes me. Could it possibly have been Gray?

After that it was left to Wimbledon to steal Taylor's thunder. In 1986 Dave Bassett's team was promoted to the First Division and after six games they topped the table. The following campaign, after beating West Bromwich Albion, Mansfield, Newcastle, Watford and Luton they had bombarded their way to Wembley.

14 May 1988 was long-ball football's greatest day. There's no doubt about it. It was a game of football won by a combination of tactics and sheer hard work, commitment and team spirit. There wasn't a single member of that Wimbledon team who you could say was a better footballer than his Liverpool counterpart. So how was it possible for eleven technically inferior players to win the FA Cup?

It was possible because the Wimbledon version of the long-ball game was the purest form yet devised. After becoming Dons manager in 1981, Dave Bassett took Graham Taylor's Watford model a step further. He refined football to its most basic form yet, and in the space of five years he had taken Wimbledon from the Fourth Division to the First.

Bassett told his team that he didn't want them to pass the ball in midfield. He didn't want them to play the ball across the back. He didn't want the goalkeeper to roll the ball out to his full backs. Ever. He wanted it launched up the pitch to the edge of the opposition's penalty area every time. It was incredible. They were at their most dangerous when goalkeeper Dave Beasant had the ball in his hands. He created most of their chances. They would pass it back to him from the centre circle and even from inside their opponents' half, so that he could pick it up and launch it back into the danger area with one of his superhuman punts.

If the ball came to the central midfielders they would just help it on. If it came to the wide midfielders they would just hurl it into the penalty area. Then up front they had two strikers who fought for everything and fed off the scraps created when all hell broke loose in the penalty area. The idea was to get the ball bouncing around their opponents' box and get someone to force it home. With their long-ball attack they would force throw-in after throw-in and corner after corner and simply launch the ball back into the box. It was simplicity itself but other teams hated it. Imagine playing against it. If you were a central defender you headed the ball more times against Wimbledon than you would in five matches against other teams.

The Wimbledon players all knew their jobs. They didn't look for great footballers in the central midfield area, they looked for commitment, drive and the ability to get forward. That was the Wimbledon way. It was raw and it was basic and a trip to their primitive old Plough Lane ground, with its tiny, damp, non-league dressing rooms and rickety wooden stands right next to the pitch, must have been about as appealing as a Vinnie Jones boot in the head. And the visiting players knew they would probably get that as well.

On top of that, of course, Wimbledon had an incredible team spirit. They were a bunch of players with a lower-league mentality who had probably thought that they would never get the chance to play at Craven Cottage, let alone Wembley, who suddenly found themselves on this rollercoaster of an adventure. The atmosphere in the dressing room was like a bunch of mates from a pub team winning the lottery and buying their way into the Premiership. There were no stars in the team, and Dave Bassett – a former player at the club who was a mate turned manager to most of the players in the early days – must take a lot of credit for fostering the incredible atmosphere. And when Bobby Gould took over in 1987 he was shrewd enough not to change it.

The players were like a close-knit family. They trained together, they played together, they went to the pub together and they got up to outrageous antics together. If they weren't leaving players stranded naked at motorway service stations, trashing each other's hotel rooms or letting each other's tyres down then they were either asleep or playing football. Talk to any sports psychologist and he will tell you the value of team spirit. Wimbledon were a team in which the players would die for each other, off the pitch as well as on it. That enabled them to take this simplistic footballing system as far as the FA Cup Final.

Wimbledon's whole attitude was summed up when they turned up for the FA Cup semi-final against Luton (which they won 2–1) in a mini-bus driven by manager Bobby Gould. The doorman wouldn't let them in – he didn't believe them when they told him who they were.

The media loved all this stuff. The Crazy Gang filled miles and miles of column inches, but no one believed they could beat Liverpool in the FA Cup Final.

The 1987/88 Liverpool side was one of the club's finest ever teams. The introduction of Peter Beardsley and John Barnes had sparked yet more from an already great team, and with the league title already in the bag this was their chance to become the first club ever to do 'the double' twice. They were the hottest favourites for the FA Cup in years. A week or so before the final they had annihilated Brian Clough's Nottingham Forest 5–0 with a performance that the great Tom Finney described as the greatest he had ever seen by any football team. Everyone thought that Wimbledon would have no chance on the wide open spaces of Wembley.

But the London team had other ideas. In many ways they had nothing to lose, but their burning desire and inner belief meant that nothing less than victory would do. In typical fashion they spent the night before the game mingling with supporters in the Fox and Grapes pub on Wimbledon Common, and they began the battle for supremacy over the league champions in the Wembley tunnel before the game. Their screaming and shouting, led by the shaven-headed Vinnie Jones and big John Fashanu, was as much a part of their tactics as playing with four at the back and hoofing it up to Fash the Bash. As the two teams lined up waiting for the signal to walk out, the Wimbledon team bawled and howled like wild animals. This was intimidation the like of which the famous old stadium had never seen before. Liverpool were used to scaring the hell out of teams just by standing there; just one look at those red shirts and famous faces was usually enough. But this time Wimbledon were letting them know they were going to have to fight for supremacy.

Both teams played a 4–4–2 formation in the final, but, in fact, their systems couldn't have been more different. Liverpool's ball-playing defence – consisting of Steve Nichol, Gary Gillespie, Gary Ablett and Alan Hansen – was the platform for all their play. They wanted the ball at their feet. It was from here that the neat little passes into people like John Barnes, Peter Beardsley and Steve McMahon would be threaded. Wimbledon's defenders, of course, were quite the opposite.

They were there to stop attacks and either hoof the ball back up the pitch or give it to Beasant so he could hoof it there.

Wimbledon played a 4–4–2 formation when they were defending, but it was more of a 4–2–4 when they were attacking (figure 61). They knew that when Beasant had the ball he would just launch it up the pitch. It would by-pass the midfield so the two wide midfielders, Dennis Wise and Alan Cork, just went straight up front to join in the fun. There was no point in them standing around in midfield and watching the ball fly over.

John Fashanu and Terry Gibson were the outlet up front for the Dons. They knew that whenever any Wimbledon player got the ball they were going to be in the action right away. So they always had to be prepared for the ball arriving up the field. But they also had to be the first line of defence, harrying and hassling the Liverpool players on the ball, to prevent them getting into their stride. Fashanu probably made more tackles in this match than any other Wimbledon player, he was like a centre back playing up front. I think he only had one shot on goal in the whole game.

Cork and Wise were wide midfielders on paper, but it wasn't their job to play as wingers. They were wide midfield players who worked up and down the whole length of the pitch. When Grobbelaar had the ball they would push forward on the Liverpool back four to make a 4–2–4 formation. They put a man on every red-shirted defender so that the Liverpool keeper was forced to kick it long. When that happened they fancied their centre backs' chances in the air over John Aldridge and Peter Beardsley more than they did if Hansen or Gillespie had the ball at their feet. Most teams were so afraid of Liverpool that as soon as Grobbelaar got the ball they would drop right back to make sure they had everyone in place in midfield. But this played right into Liverpool's hands because it meant that players like Hansen had time on the ball to pick out their passes and stroll out with the ball (figure 62). By cutting off this supply Wimbledon cut out a huge part of what had made Liverpool such a great side.

If Liverpool did get hold of the ball then Wise and Cork would drop back in to make it 4–4–2 in the traditional way. And when they won the ball in the last third they simply launched it into the box.

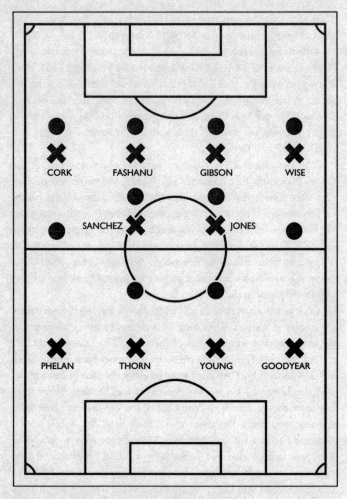

Figure 61: How Wimbledon's 1988 cup-winning team converted from 4–4–2 to 4–2–4 when Dave Beasant was about to launch one of his huge kicks

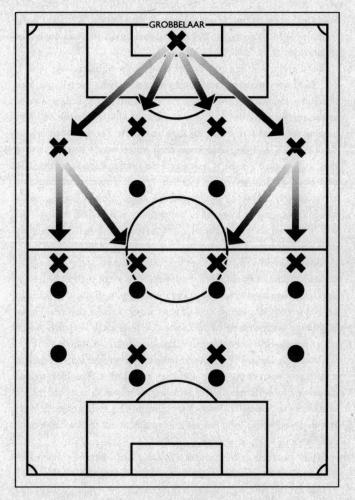

Figure 62: How Liverpool would normally have built their attacks, starting with a throw-out from the goalkeeper

Someone worked out before the match that Dennis Wise had been responsible for seventy-five per cent of their goals that season, either as provider or as the scorer himself.

For Lawrie Sanchez and Vinnie Jones in the middle of the park it was all about competing and contesting and helping the ball on. You never saw those two getting the ball down and playing little one-twos in the centre of midfield. It was a question of winning the ball and helping it forward, that was all they had to do. The whole team was so disciplined and everyone knew their job. It was a way of playing that was worked on the training ground until it became natural. So that when the ball arrived in a certain area in a match situation they knew exactly where to put it and the other players knew exactly where it was going. They could almost play blind when they got the ball into certain areas because the system had been so heavily drummed into them.

Bobby Gould had taken over from Dave Bassett at the start of the season, and he recognised what an incredible set of players he had at the club, and changed nothing. The only thing he did was to bring in his old friend Don Howe, one of the country's finest coaches. Howe is credited with coming up with the one little tactical switch which many people believe enabled the Dons to win this match.

Normally Dennis Wise would have played on the left of midfield and Alan Cork on the right. But they switched it. The idea was to cancel out John Barnes on the right. Barnes was in the form of his life and Howe realised that Dennis's mobility and his ability to get around the pitch and hassle John Barnes' legs could cut out the source of most of Liverpool's attacking play.

That was their gamble and it worked a treat. Barnes' influence in the game wasn't great as Wise stopped him playing. He niggled away at him for the whole game like a little terrier, no doubt giving him a dose of the old cheeky cockney verbals for the entire ninety minutes, and simply didn't allow him to play. Barnes was a shadow of the player he had been all season.

As the game went on it became clear that Liverpool weren't clicking. Wimbledon simply didn't let them get into their rhythm. As Liverpool couldn't get the ball on the floor at the back and because they were being closed down so hard Grobbelaar was punting it long, straight down the throats of Wimbledon's centre backs Andy Thorn and Eric Young, who just lapped it up. Barnes was stifled by Wise, Vinnie Jones (whose 'welcome to the game' tackle on Steve McMahon was like something off Hackney Marshes) and Lawrie Sanchez blocked up the middle of the park and the defence stood firm. There were a couple of shaky moments in the first half, notably when Beardsley had the ball in the net only for play to be called back for a Liverpool free kick, but it wasn't a siege by any means and with their 'route one' strategy Wimbledon always posed a threat.

That threat materialised in the thirty-sixth minute when Lawrie Sanchez nodded in Dennis Wise's free kick to make it 1–0. Of course, there was Beasant's penalty save from John Aldridge in the second half but it was a harsh decision by referee Brian Hill in the first place and, apart from that, Liverpool really had very few chances. They had been out-psyched, out-fought and out-thought by Wimbledon, a club which had been a member of the Football League for only eleven years. It was a great story. When Bobby Gould got home with the FA Cup after a long and boozy night at Plough Lane he found that he still had the FA Cup with him. He didn't know what to do with it, so he slept with it in his bed.

If your team is not littered with great players, then you've got to go with what you have. Wimbledon had to play this way because they didn't have the quality players that Liverpool had. They weren't able to buy them. So they got a bunch of players and told them that long-ball football was the only way that they could get success. Long-ball football evolved because it was a way in which less talented teams could compete against, and beat, better teams. Wimbledon would ask questions of defenders right from the first minute. They would ask the opposition how good they were, how strong they were and how much they wanted to win. It was as simple as that.

The psychology of their game was a huge part of their success. They psyched out Liverpool, I don't think there's a doubt about that. They imposed themselves at every opportunity – for example, the tackle by Vinnie on Steve McMahon, the talking, the verbals. In 1988 Wimbledon were all about putting people under pressure. It was direct football. If the full back got the ball, it was going down the line and into the corner. If he got it further forward then it was going in the box. If it bounced in the middle of the park it was hooked over the top. There was no thought of pulling the ball down and making a short pass.

Wimbledon built on the fact that teams would drop back when they played them and defend from deep because they knew the long ball was coming. But when you did that against Wimbledon they were happy because it meant they could push right up on top of you on the edge of the box. Then if anything dropped down in that area, they were in with a good chance of creating an opportunity to score. A lot of teams played straight into their hands. I think that you had to be brave against them. You had to hold the line and say, 'Go on, then. Play it over the top and let's see if you're good enough to spring our offside trap.'

In fact we won the championship at Everton playing a kind of mixture of long ball and passing. It wasn't Liverpool and it wasn't Wimbledon. We had people like me and Graeme Sharp up front and when you've got people who are big, strong and good in the air in the forward line you have to use it. It's a waste of time passing it about at the back when your threat is at the other end. So we tried to get it forward to Graeme Sharpe as often as possible and often by hitting a long ball. We would knock it to the edge of the box and Sharpey and I would try to get it down and play it. But we wouldn't always do it. We weren't as obvious as Wimbledon. Wimbledon only had one way to play. But we did were pretty direct at Everton at times.

People said after the 1988 FA Cup Final that Liverpool had just played badly that day but I don't subscribe to that view. I don't think that people should take anything away from Wimbledon. For twenty years Liverpool had been passing the ball about, but these upstarts from non-league got it down and then whacked it forward into the danger areas. They rode their luck at times, but you always need luck in cup finals.

The team spirit was vital for Wimbledon. I played in teams that won games because of their great team spirit. It's all about a group of players getting on together, on and off the pitch. I think that most good teams will have a bunch of lads that get on well together. At Everton in the mid-1980s we had maybe thirteen or fourteen lads who went to the pub together and had a good night out. That kind of camaraderie and spirit is important.

It's a manager's job to try to create team spirit. Dave Bassett simply allowed it to evolve naturally, he had a laugh and joke and let the players get away with things that you simply couldn't at a big club. When I was at Everton Howard Kendall used to take all of us away as a unit. We would have a load of beers, a big Chinese meal and stay in the restaurant for five or six hours, having a good laugh and a joke, and we did that two or three times a year. Maybe modern managers wouldn't think it important, but I think it's a crucial aspect of the game.

The reason that long-ball football has faded from the game is that people have begun to realise that it can only take you so far. In one-off situations it gives you a chance, which is how Wimbledon managed to win the FA Cup, but it could never win you the league. It could never win you a trophy in Europe because you need more. Route one football gives you just one option, one mode of attack, so if things aren't going right, if the defence against which you are launching your assaults is big and strong and prepared for the battle then you have no plan B. You will end up banging your head against a brick wall. Eventually you will come up against teams who will head the ball and compete with you but won't fold. Look at the modern Manchester United. And that's when you need something else. With Wimbledon in 1988, there simply wasn't anything else.

That's why the modern Wimbledon have changed under Joe Kinnear. They have softened. They are still very direct but the modern Wimbledon play a lot more in that last third than the 1988 side did. They have got players like Michael Hughes and Neal Ardley who can get the ball down and probe at defences and create chances without always just humping it into the box. They have adapted and evolved, just as football has done.

CHAPTER 15
Setpieces

There was a time in the game when teams would just toss in a corner or a free kick without much thought. Up until the 1970s games were so open they were likely to be littered with chances, so winning a corner or a free kick was far less crucial than it is today. These days, if you look at the statistics, the number of goals scored from setpieces is incredible – something like forty-five per cent of goals come from corners, free kicks or long throws – as is the amount of planning that goes into their execution.

As defences just keep getting stronger and better organised, setpieces have become more important than ever before. In the modern game they can be your only chance of even getting close to scoring and today's coaches are spending more and more time on the training pitch, wracking their brains to come up with new routines to outfox their opponents.

For a coach, planning a setpiece is one of the few times when you can transfer the tactics board directly onto the pitch. He can actually put his players on the pitch in the exact positions he has worked out on paper, something that simply can't happen when the ball is in open play. Designing setpieces has become like a science with people such as Terry Venables and Howard Wilkinson the pioneers of the craft.

In a setpiece situation within thirty yards of the goal it is possible to put more men in the box than is realistically possible at any time in open play. A team can put six or seven men in the box if they like. In open play that would be suicidal, but you can do it at a setpiece.

Just think how often a tight game has been opened up or won by a setpiece. One fairly recent occasion which springs to mind is when England played Moldova at home in the World Cup qualifying tournament for France '98. England huffed and puffed for thirty minutes without getting anywhere but it was a game they simply had to win. They were playing an inferior side but one which was well organised. It wasn't until they got a corner that they looked like scoring, Paul Scholes heading home after Paul Gascoigne's inswinger was only half-cleared. Ten years ago England would have thrashed a side like Moldova, but teams are now so much more disciplined that that simply doesn't happen. After Scholes's goal the game opened up and England went on to win 4–0, but that first goal was crucial.

It's not just the number of people who you can pile into the box for setpieces that make them so dangerous, it's the fact that you can pick and choose exactly who goes where. You can put your personnel where you want. It's not like open play where someone might find themselves in an awkward area where they're not comfortable. At a corner, for instance, you can put both your centre backs who are good in the air up as well as your centre forward. At what stage in open play will you ever get the three players who pose your biggest aerial threat in the box waiting to get on the end of a cross? Never. When, apart from at a corner or free kick, would Arsenal ever get Tony Adams, Steve Bould and Martin Keown in the penalty area together as a high ball comes in? It just doesn't happen, yet think of the number of goals they've got between them from corners for the Gunners over the last ten years.

The most vital thing is the delivery of the ball. Every team needs a midfielder or a full back who can whip in a dangerous ball from anywhere in the attacking third of the pitch. It shouldn't be a problem. I can't think of a Premiership side which doesn't have at least one player capable of getting a ball up and over a wall and down again.

When it comes to free kicks the hard thing is coming up with something new, because almost everything has been tried before. Creating that element of surprise is harder and harder. A manager will sit down with his coaches and jot down a few ideas. Then they will go out on the training ground, probably using the kids from the youth team to try out their ideas. The coaches must work out how they can create a bit of space where they might find a little opening.

Manchester United executed a great free kick against Chelsea in the 1997/98 FA Cup. The kick was about thirty yards out, just to the right of the goal, and so obviously Chelsea lined up a wall of five or six players. United put Teddy Sheringham on the end of the wall, next to Dan Petrescu who was covering De Goey's left-hand post. Then, as David Beckham ran up to shoot – aiming just inside that left-hand post – Sheringham grabbed hold of Petrescu and pulled him out of the way. The ball flew through the gap and into the net. Technically Sheringham was fouling Petrescu, but because the referee was lined up on the other side of the wall they got away with it (figure 63).

Another free kick you'll often see around the edge of the box is one which gives the player striking the ball an angle to beat the wall. If the ball is on the left-hand side of the goal the attacking team puts a man just a few yards to the left of the ball. The player taking the free kick just rolls the ball to this player. He stops it while another player runs up to blast his shot. By working this little triangle they have worked an angle that by-passes the wall and has the chance of stranding the goalkeeper who is probably on the other side of the goal expecting a chip into the corner (figure 64).

Another routine from about the same sort of position which is even more deceptive than this requires a more delicate touch of craft. Imagine the ball is lined up outside the box, this time on the right, and again the opposition lines up its wall. The attacking team puts a man on the right-hand end of the wall and another right on the edge of the box a few yards away from the wall. Then the player taking the free kick runs up and shapes to shoot, but instead fires in a low pass to the player on the edge of the box. This player then plays a little diagonal pass in behind the wall from which the attacking player who was stationed on the end has spun off. If the pass is right he will be clean through on goal (figure 65).

We used to have a great free-kick routine when I was playing for Scotland which, when it worked, could have had some of the key players up for Oscars. If we had a free kick in a wide area on the edge of the box, two players would stand over the ball and four of us would run in. Now as we began to run into the box the two players over the ball would pretend to make a mess of the kick, they would run up to the ball and stop as if they were confused as to who was

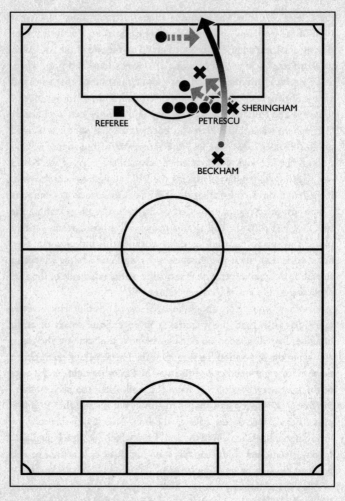

Figure 63: Beckham's free kick against Chelsea

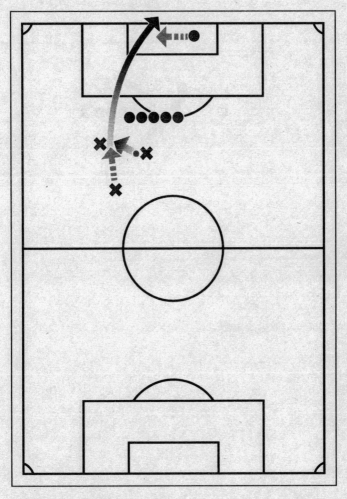

Figure 64: Working an angle around a wall

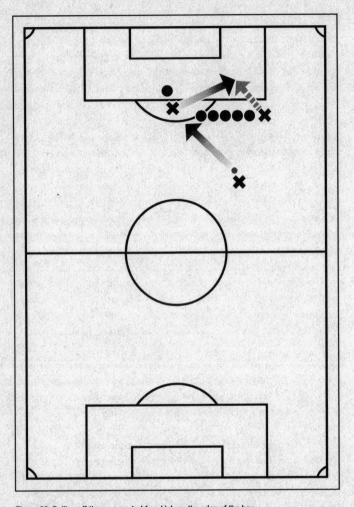

Figure 65: Pulling off the unexpected free kick on the edge of the box

going to take it. They would then start arguing, and as soon as they did this our markers would stop. They would relax their concentration for a second, thinking we were going to re-group. We forwards would start to walk back then suddenly spin back in, just as one of the players on the ball chipped it into the box. If it worked it meant that the entire defence would be taken completely by surprise and one of us would have a free header.

There was another one we did at Villa when the ball was going to come into the box from wide. I would line up at the edge of the box, and two of my team-mates would line up in front of me, nearer the goal. Just as the ball was about to be played, these two would turn, and run straight at my marker. This was the signal for the man taking the free kick to play the ball into the middle. So as I went around the outside of the group of players my marker would be blocked, quite legally, by my team-mates, leaving me with a free header right in the centre of goal (figure 66).

Good managers will let players come up with suggestions about how to improvise. Often they have great imagination, they're actually out there and can see what's going on. Sometimes you can only get away with a free kick once. A lot of clubs will have a free-kick routine up their sleeve which they save for a big game. The kick will look brand new but will have been worked on at the training ground. There's no point letting the cat out of the bag in a game you're already winning 3–0. Keep it for an important match. Once you've announced it to the world, it's there for all to see and then it's doubly difficult to do it again.

I remember one setpiece which worked time and time again for Tottenham a few years ago and I couldn't believe that teams kept letting them do it. At corners Darren Anderton would fire in an outswinger with his right foot which would fly to about level with the near post but twelve to fifteen yards out. Teddy Sheringham would line up at the near post but, just as the kick was being played, he would step out and when the ball came to him he would volley it home (figure 67). I watched them do this time and time again and I remember pointing it out on *The Boot Room*, the tactics show I was doing on Sky Sports at the time. The Spurs manager, Gerry Francis,

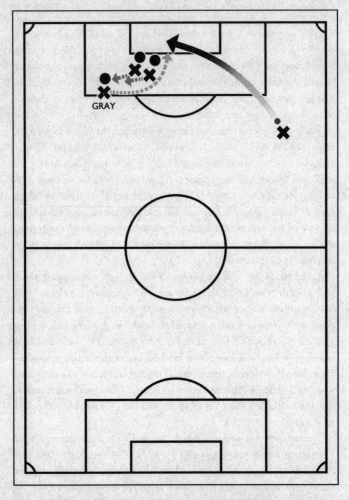

Figure 66: The Aston Villa free kick where my marker would be blocked by my team-mates as the cross came in

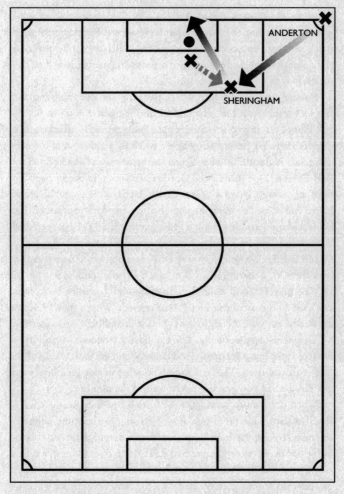

Figure 67: Tottenham's successful corner kick involving Anderton and Sheringham

wrote to me saying: 'Please Andy it's hard enough to score goals without you telling the nation what we're up to.' But if I could see it, surely everyone else could. Mind you, it's testimony to the quality of the delivery from Anderton and the finish by Sheringham that they could do it time and time again.

Having gone on about forwards planning and designing intricate free kicks, there is a lot to be said for the one where you just put the ball down, put it into the danger area and get people attacking it in the air. There's a famous story about when Don Howe went to Leeds as a coach in the 1970s when Leeds had great players like Eddie Gray, Billy Bremner, Joe Jordan and Gordon McQueen. In one of their first training sessions Don, who is a master tactician, got out the blackboard and started running through this new free-kick routine. He had his blackboard and his chalk and he marked it all up. He then said, 'Eddie Gray, you're A; Billy Bremner, you're B; Johnny Giles, you're C; and Gordon McQueen, you're D. Now what we do here is A runs over the ball, dummies it for B to give to C who puts in a cross for D.' The players stood around murmuring until someone said: 'Don, can't we do the usual free kick?' Don replied: 'What's that?' And the answer he got was: 'Well, Jonesie chips it in and big Gordon scores.'

That sums it up perfectly. You can have a wonderful imagination for free kicks but sometimes good delivery and good attacking of the ball is all you need. The real issue is whether or not the players can put those ideas into practice in the heat of the moment.

When it comes to scoring direct from a free kick on the edge of the area then, nine times out of ten, it's simply about the ability of the man striking the ball. When we were winning things at Everton in the 1980s we were fortunate to have Kevin Sheedy on our side, a player who had the most exquisite left foot I have ever seen. He could basically do anything he wanted with the ball. I remember when we played Ipswich in a cup tie at Goodison. We got a free kick just outside the box and, while they were lining up their wall, Kevin thought he heard the referee say he could take it so he bent the ball into the goalie's top left-hand corner. But the referee hadn't blown so he had to take it again. This time Kevin stepped up and put it in the other corner. It was unbelievable.

He could deliver the ball from left or right – outswinger or inswinger – which meant that the opposition didn't know if he was going to cross or shoot. We didn't really work on free kicks then because we knew exactly what would happen in every situation and we knew that the delivery was so good we wouldn't have to do anything fancy. If we were central we knew Sheeds would shoot. If it was indirect we knew the ball would get shifted to either Kevin or Trevor Steven to hit.

You can never play for a free kick. You can't make a tactical decision that, because you've got Zola in the team, you will play a certain way to try to get free kicks around the box. I think players will get the ball into certain areas and if there's body contact they will go down like a ton of bricks, but that's just the nature of the modern game. I don't think a front player when it's played up to him ever goes down because he knows he's got Zola, Juninho or Beckham in his team. I don't think in the heat of the battle you're ever thinking that far ahead.

In the era of the long-ball game, however, teams certainly played for corner kicks. Teams like Watford and Wimbledon knew that by knocking it long into the corners they might not get a goalscoring chance but there was a good chance of winning a corner off a panicky defender.

Corner-kick tactics themselves have changed dramatically over the years. Not so long ago pretty much the only corner kick you ever really saw was the outswinger. The ball would be curled away from the keeper with people running from the edge of the box to attack it. There was the inswinger too, a ball which curved in to right under the crossbar to put the goalkeeper under real pressure, but that was about as imaginative as it got. Basically if you won a corner kick on the right-hand side, you could either have a right-footed player take it and the natural curve of the ball when he struck it would bend it away from the goalkeeper, or you put a left footer on it and he would bend it in towards goal.

The introduction of the near-post corner, however, added a whole new dimension to the game. Often effective and hard to defend, the near-post corner is lethal if the delivery is good and those going for the ball are big, strong and brave. As far as I can remember, it first emerged in the early 1980s and it's a tactic that we've exploited in this country more than anywhere else in the world. The Italians weren't interested in it for years and have only recently realised its importance.

The tactic is to put in two big men at the near post. Then the opposition has to put three in there with them, two markers and one protecting the near post itself. That means that as the corner is taken you have got five players congested at the near post. The idea, then, is to fire the ball in where the six-yard line meets the touchline, drop it into that area with pace, and hope that it is flicked on – either by your player or even off the head of a defender stretching to reach the ball – across goal.

This second ball then becomes virtually impossible to defend. As forwards rush in towards it it is much easier for them, with their forward momentum, to put the ball into the goal than it is for the defence to defend. The goalkeeper, too, is likely to be stranded since as the initial ball comes in he must cover the near post in case the ball is headed straight in towards goal.

Arsenal became masters of the near-post corner under George Graham. It seemed that every corner they got was banged in to Steve Bould at the near post with half the Arsenal team charging into the six-yard box behind him. There was a spell during the late 1980s and early 1990s that every corner we ever saw in England was dropped in at the near post, and when you look at its success rate I suppose that's not surprising.

The other thing that teams seem to like playing at the moment is little short corners. Chelsea do it all the time, where Zola will knock it two or three yards to Wise, Wise will stop it, and Zola will then fire the ball in from there. All it means is that he is playing the cross a couple of yards nearer the goal and a couple of yards back from the by-line. I can't really see why they do it. The difference in the angle they get for the cross is so small that it doesn't seem worth it, especially as it gives defenders a chance to get in and block the cross. The only thing I can think of is that they're hoping to score. In other words, if Zola whips in the ball wickedly and no one gets a touch it will go straight into the back of the net.

The long throw is another set play which has emerged as an important weapon in the armoury of some teams. If they have a player capable of hurling the ball from the touchline into the box sides will use the tactic much to the same effect as they would a near-post corner. They will fire the ball in towards the near post and hope that someone can get a flick on it and flash the ball across the face of goal. There's no great strategy or finesse about it, but if you've got someone like Vinnie Jones or Gary Neville in your team then why not hurl the ball into the box and see what happens.

One of the best setpiece goals I've ever witnessed, however, didn't involve any tactical trickery or movement off the ball. It was simply a glorious shot from one of the best free-kick takers the world has ever seen: Brazil's Roberto Carlos. Early on in the first game of *Le Tournoi de France* in 1997 Brazil got a free kick against France, about thirty yards from goal. The French goalkeeper set up his wall, but he hadn't accounted for Carlos' lethal left foot. The Real Madrid left back took a monster run-up and smashed the ball with the outside of his boot. I don't think I've ever seen a football curl so much as it curved around the wall and then back into the corner of the net. That wasn't great imagination or planning, it was just an amazing piece of skill.

CHAPTER 16
England 1997

● ●

ITALY 0 ENGLAND 0
11 October 1997 (World Cup Qualifier)
Olympic Stadium, Rome. Attendance: 80,000

England: (5–3–2)

Seaman

Beckham   Campbell   Adams   Southgate   Le Saux

Gascoigne   Ince   Batty

Sheringham   Wright

Italy: Peruzzi, Nesta, Maldini, Albertini, Cannavaro, Costacurta, Di
Livio, D Baggio, Vieri, Zola, Inzaghi

*With the whole nation holding its breath, Glenn Hoddle's team
needed just a point from their final group game to qualify for France
'98. But Italy had never had any result other than a win in any World
Cup game played at the Olympic Stadium so it was going to be one
hell of a point to earn. Still, despite a fiercely passionate crowd and
with the added distraction of riot police wading into their supporters
for much of the first half, England kept their cool and controlled the
game. Italy had a couple of early chances when Ince was off the pitch
having a head wound stitched, but the loss of the Italian manager's
son, attacking left back Paolo Maldini – with an ankle injury – was
a huge blow to the men in blue. As the game went on England began
to dominate possession more and more and they carved out the two*

best opportunities of the half, Ince's shot being saved well by Peruzzi and Beckham's going just over the bar. In the second half it was more of the same, with Italy struggling to break through England's packed midfield. The home side's frustration was getting the better of them and when Di Livio lunged at Sol Campbell to earn his second yellow card of the game and an automatic sending off it was surely all over. In the fourth minute of injury time it simply had to be when Ian Wright broke free and rounded the keeper, but his shot hit the post. Immediately Italy broke down the other end, for the first time in the match stretching the England defence. The ball was crossed in but Vieri, free in the middle, headed wide.

As far as I am concerned England are now one of the top six sides in world football, and a big part of that has to go down to the tactical revolution started by Terry Venables and continued admirably by Glenn Hoddle. These two England managers are responsible for bringing the England team out of the dark ages. In the space of the last four years first Venables and then Hoddle have successfully adapted the traditional qualities of the English game – passion, pace and power – to the more refined needs of the international stage. England now have a team which can compete with the best, a team that at times seems to be playing a totally different game to the one Graham Taylor's side played as they failed to qualify for the 1994 World Cup in the USA. Forget sweeper systems and deep-lying strikers for a moment, forget diamond midfields and defending from the front, both Venables and Hoddle based their entire philosophy on the simple fact that in international football you have to be able to keep the ball.

Possession, they say, is nine tenths of the law, well in international football it's ten tenths. It's crucial. Teams are so organised that it is incredibly hard to score a goal, so the longer you can keep possession of the ball the more questions you can ask of your opponent. And as the play is generally of a much higher standard than club football, if you let the other team have the ball then it's hard to get it back.

This was the secret of England's famous World Cup qualification-clinching 0–0 draw. By winning the ball, holding onto it and then passing it patiently around the midfield, England killed the game off. Hoddle's side had long spells of possession in the match where the Italians were charging around trying to get it back off them, draining themselves physically and mentally. A lot of the time England weren't necessarily going anywhere with their passing but they knew that if they had the ball the Italians couldn't hurt them.

The ability to keep the ball distinguishes the current England side from the national sides of the last twenty years or so. Of course, the cautious, slow build-up style of play in Rome was shaped by the need only to secure a draw, but keeping possession is the secret whether you need to draw 0–0 or win 3–0. Only when you have the ball can you step up the pace of your game if you need a goal, only when you have the ball can you hurt your opponents and be sure that they can't hurt you.

Glenn Hoddle's England team plays, invariably, with a back five – three central defenders and two wing backs. It's the system that Hoddle has persevered with throughout his managerial career, from Swindon to Chelsea to England. It's five at the back when the opposition is attacking, but as soon as England have the ball it's three at the back as the wing backs surge forward. Add to this three central midfielders and two strikers – one playing deep, in 'the hole' – and that's Glenn's system. Call it 3–5–2 or 5–3–2, call it what you like, because I don't think that the system is the main secret of England's recent resurgence, it's more the style of play that Venables and Hoddle have developed.

At international level a manager can choose the system which he wants to play and then pick his players accordingly. It's not a case of building a system around the particular players he's got. Glenn is comfortable with this system as a manager, he's chosen to implement it at international level and I believe the players are now comfortable playing this way (even though most play entirely different systems with their clubs). But I am equally sure that another manager could come along, take charge of this England squad and play four at the back quite comfortably.

Glenn's system keeps it strong in the middle, right down the centre of the pitch. When you have three traditional centre backs they pretty much stay in position for the whole game. In the same way if you go for three in midfield then for most of the game you've got good cover in front of your defence. If there is a problem with this then I think it's that you can get exposed out wide. The wing backs – against Italy it was David Beckham on the right and Graeme Le Saux on the left – are your only real wide players on the pitch which means they must shore up the defence, support in midfield and, whenever possible, get forward and support the attack. That's one hell of a job.

The one thing that I was worried about before the game from England's point of view was that Italian left back Paolo Maldini – probably the best attacking left back in the world – would have a lot of joy down England's right-hand side. The thing is that although Beckam has got immense qualities, I'm not sure how many of those qualities are defensive, and I wondered whether Hoddle might have been tempted to play Beckham's Manchester United colleague Gary Neville, a traditional right back, instead of him in that right wing back position. Since England only needed a draw I thought he might take this more cautious approach.

And in fact, early on in the game, Maldini got a lot of the ball down that left side and caused England some problems, pushing Beckham right back for much of the first fifteen minutes or so. I think Gary Neville would have been better equipped to cope with Maldini because of his defensive ability.

Fortunately for England, Maldini went off injured after about half an hour of the game. It was a massive, massive bonus for Glenn Hoddle. Early on Gianfranco Zola, who was playing as a third, deeplying striker for the Italians, was linking up with Maldini on the right wing and they were doubling up on Beckham. Now that looked a threat because Sol Campbell was getting dragged out to the right to help Beckham out which meant there were several occasions early on when Adams and Southgate were two against two in the box against the two main Italian strikers, Vieri and Inzaghi. The whole point about five at the back is supposed to be that your defenders always outnumber the strikers, but that wasn't happening. Had Maldini not gone off I don't know what would have happened, but there were a couple of scares early on when the Italian left back got into dangerous areas and fired in some decent balls and it's something I'm sure Glenn must have been concerned about.

In fact, Glenn must have been aware of the potential risk from the Italian left because of the way he lined up the back three. As I have mentioned, he anchored the back three with Tony Adams in the middle, flanking him with Sol Campbell on the right and Gareth Southgate on the left. Now of the three, Tony is probably the least mobile, so it made sense to put him in the middle and have two quicker players on either side of him. He put Sol Campbell, probably the quickest of the three, on the right which meant that he could get across and cover for Beckham when he was under pressure.

Before the game I had assumed that England would play with two holding midfielders in this game in Batty and Ince and that's exactly what they did. Both these players can sit in front of the defence and protect it. They're both good spoilers, able to get a foot in and break up the opposition's momentum, but they are good passers of the ball too. So you had those two sitting quite deep in front of the defence which left Paul Gascoigne up ahead of them to go and influence the game, to get involved a bit more and link up with Sheringham and Wright.

The object for England was to give nothing away but still to try to create openings at the other end. So Teddy Sheringham's role, playing as a deep striker behind Ian Wright, was crucial. He was expected to link up with Wright in attack but also to drop into midfield and help deny them space, to become England's fourth midfielder whenever they didn't have the ball.

Wrighty knew that he had to work his socks off. When the ball came up to him he had to try and hold it up as much as possible. He had to hold the ball and bring the support players like Sheringham and Gascoigne into the play as much as possible. He had to buy England some time. Having a striker who can hold the ball while he gets support is vital in this system – it's something that Shearer does so well – because it's crucial to retaining possession. If the ball is cleared from defence and all the striker can do is flick it on to the opposition goalkeeper there's no respite for the defence. The opposition are back on the attack again right away. Holding the ball and then keeping it is all about relieving the pressure, both physically and, in a contest as intense as this, mentally.

Glenn wasn't too worried if the Italians fired crosses into the box from deep, wide areas. He felt that with Adams, Campbell and Southgate – all big men and good in the air – that that would just be playing into England's hands. Although Hoddle knew they had Vieri of Atletico Madrid who is big and tall and a good header of the ball, he thought he had the players to deal with that threat. What he didn't want was the likes of Zola zipping around just in front of Adams, Campbell and Southgate, slipping little balls through and playing one-twos on the edge of the area.

So England kept the space between the three centre backs and Ince and Batty down to a minimum when they didn't have the ball (figures 68a and b). This meant that Zola had great difficulty finding space in that area where he thrives. Where he did find space was further out wide, in front of Ince and Batty, but they never allowed him to come inside where he could really hurt England – either by shooting for goal himself or by sliding little balls into the box for Vieri or Inzaghi.

The job of the midfield three that night was a simple one. Their job was to deny the Italians space, not so much by tackling but by standing up, getting back in and denying them room just in front of the three central defenders. They were there to spoil. Then, when they got the ball their job was to keep it and use it well. For long spells England kept the ball in midfield, not really going anywhere but slowly killing the game off, frustrating the Italians. Then they would slip a ball into the forwards on the off chance of creating something at the other end.

Paul Gascoigne would have been told to drop back and help close down the space when England didn't have the ball. But he would also have been instructed that, when England did have it, to try and commit players and open something up. By pushing forward and making things happen Glenn wanted him to buy his team some time and give the defence a breather.

And it must be said that the whole plan worked perfectly. England had very few scares in the game which is remarkable when you consider that Italy had a hundred per cent record of victories in World

Figure 68(a)

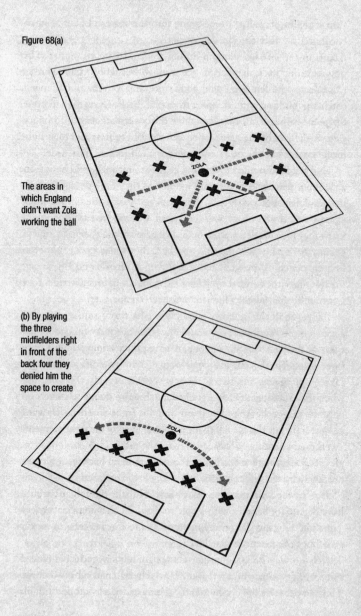

The areas in which England didn't want Zola working the ball

(b) By playing the three midfielders right in front of the back four they denied him the space to create

Cup matches played in Rome going into the match, David Seaman becoming the first foreign goalkeeper not to concede a goal to the *Azzuri* in the famous stadium during a World Cup encounter. The only time that the Italians really got through was when Maldini broke clear down the left-hand side when Ince was off the pitch having stitches in his head wound. Apart from that there was no need to press the panic button until that incredible thirty seconds deep into injury time at the end of the game when Wright hit the post and then Italy broke straight up the other end only for Vieri to head just wide.

Had England needed to win the game I think we would have seen a different team selection from Hoddle. As they only needed a draw the emphasis was purely and simply on not losing. But it can work against you if you know you only need a draw. In 1989 Liverpool knew they only needed a point in the last game of the season at Anfield against Arsenal to win the title – in fact, they knew they could even lose the match by one goal and still end up as champions. By playing for the draw they ended up losing the game 2–0, and the title, to a last-minute goal by the Gunners' Michael Thomas.

But psychologically, when you only need a draw, it does make you a touch more cautious. You would always make sure you had a man spare at the back. If your opponents have got two up you must have three back. That's your insurance policy. You wouldn't want to get caught one against one, two against two or three against three because when the other team needs a goal so much more than you there's no need to take a gamble. Beckham and Le Saux could go forward against Italy but it was vital that they chose exactly the right moment, when they knew there was cover from the midfield. You don't stop players going forward and if a goal comes it comes, but you don't give one away by chasing the game.

Due to the way that they play their football, the Italians would have been a lot happier with a role reversal. In Italy they start every game like England did on the night of 11 October, hoping to nick a goal but concentrating first and foremost on not giving one away. There's no way Italian manager Cesare Maldini would have picked three strikers – Inzaghi, Vieri and Zola – if he had needed a 0–0 draw. You can bet your life on that. Had Glenn needed a win I don't think he would have gone in with both Ince and Batty in the same team. He would probably have gone in with Ince and possibly Scholes alongside Gascoigne in midfield.

England did to Italy that night what Italy have done to so many teams over the years. Italy know how to set up a quality defence that's well drilled, well disciplined and knows its job, and now England have shown that they do too. In the past England have always gone out and tried to win the game when playing crucial away games in Italy. In a 1976 World Cup qualifier they ended up losing 2–0 in Rome and during the 1980 European Championship they lost 1–0 in Turin. I think that technically, tactically and psychologically, five years ago an England team would not have been able to get this result in Rome. The England side then did not have a manager instilling in them the belief that they could go out on a pitch somewhere like the Olympic Stadium and pass and keep the ball. Under Graham Taylor the understanding was that if you were a full back and you had the ball you hit it long. Under Glenn Hoddle the instruction is clear: keep the ball.

It has taken four years of drilling, four years of coaching and training at Bisham Abbey. It's all about Terry Venables and Hoddle encouraging passing and movement but passing and movement with a purpose.

I don't believe that the players are technically better now than they were five or ten years ago. If you practise more then you will be more used to a system and a style and so you'll be able to execute it better, but I've always believed that British players are as technically gifted as foreign players. I've never subscribed to the theory that because you are a foreigner you are better. There are some great foreign players – like Zola – but are they really any better than Beckham or Sheringham? I would argue all day long that they're not. It's all down to the instructions from the manager. For the last four years the pattern of play for the England team has been possession with a purpose. Combine that with some seriously good players and you've got the basis for a very successful team.

On this night I don't think England had a single player who had a bad game. The back three were superb. Ince and Batty in the centre of midfield were strong. The spine of the team was strong. The members of this England side are all big-time players, they all thrive on the atmosphere. But, to a certain extent, the days of being intimidated by an atmosphere have gone now. If you play at this level it's partly because you're not intimidated by an atmosphere. If you don't want to play in big games then you shouldn't be an international.

I also think that the England players have been helped by the fact that we've got more and more foreign players in the Premiership now. English players are up against them every week. It shows them that they are as good. It's partly a psychological thing. But British clubs have always been among the best in Europe, if not the best. Before the ban which came after Heysel, whenever a European side was drawn against a British side it was the European side which was worried and I think it's getting back that way now.

Just look at the way those England players handled what was probably one of the most intimidating atmospheres they will ever play in. England had young players in the side like Beckham and Campbell but they rose to the magnitude of the occasion. That shows great strength of character and is another indication of Hoddle's influence on his players.

I wasn't surprised by how much England controlled the game in Rome. And on the other hand, even after they won at Wembley 1–0 in February of the same year I really didn't think this was a great Italian side. When I saw that Maldini had picked Vieri and Inzaghi I thought England would be OK. Although they are players with great reputations across Europe they have hardly had any international experience, and they certainly weren't proven international goalscorers. There was certainly no Paolo Rossi, Toto Schillaci or Gigi Riva out there. I thought that if the England players believed in themselves they would be able to pass the ball about and get a result.

Hoddle of course must take great, great credit. He's taken a side that for two years under Terry Venables had learned that there are different priorities at international level – you must keep possession and you must take your chances – and he's taken it a stage further.

The psychological things that Hoddle did before the game also showed how much more sophisticated he is as a coach than, say, Graham Taylor. By pulling Gareth Southgate and David Beckham out of training the day before the match and convincing the press that they were both doubtful for the game he was playing mind games with Maldini. I think it would be hard, psychologically, to affect Glenn. He's mentally strong. On the other hand, I think Maldini showed signs of agitation before the match – for example, in Italy's game against Georgia he was like a man possessed on the touchline as his players tried in vain to score a goal – and that's why I think Glenn played a few little tricks. The idea was just to put a few seeds of doubt in his mind about the composition of the England team, just to unsettle him a bit. It's part and parcel of the modern game. Not only are you going to be tested physically, but you're going to be tested mentally as well if you want to get to the very top.

I think Hoddle is bound to play his 3–5–2 system throughout the World Cup in France. It's what he likes. If I was a manager in international football I would play four at the back because that's what I like. But if he goes into the biggest match he's ever had as a manager and plays as he did in Italy, that suggests that he's always going to play this system. He might tinker with it for certain games, but not often.

The only time Hoddle's England team have ever gone into a game playing anything other than five at the back was against Moldova in the World Cup qualifier at Wembley in September 1997. On that occasion Hoddle played four at the back because there was no point in having three defenders standing around marking one forward of limited international ability. He played four in defence but with the full backs still going forward like wing backs. It wasn't actually that different. He simply sacrificed a centre back who was surplus to requirements for another forward-thinking player, namely Paul Scholes. He might do it again in the World Cup against a team like Tunisia if he thinks he can blow them away but I suspect he'll stick with five at the back. It may become a tactic England only use at Wembley against very weak teams.

I think that Hoddle is more likely to change players than his system. For example, he could play a more defensive right wing-back against a team who had a particular threat on the left. The system would be the same but the tactical approach slightly different. To combat Brazil's attacking flair he might put Gary Neville in at right wing-back to combat Denilson. But he might put Beckham into central midfield and leave out Batty so that he's got more attacking options in the central area. I think that is a genuinely good option for Hoddle. I think there might be a very strong case for playing Beckham, Ince and Gascoigne in the centre in France with Neville on the right.

Glenn's also got options up front. If fit, Shearer will almost certainly play, and then the question is whether to play Scholes or Sheringham. I don't think they will both play in the same team. They are very similar players and both ideal for that slightly deeper striking role. But if Glenn needed to get a win in a group game, he could take a chance and go for the five at the back, with Ince and Batty in midfield to shore everything up and then play Sheringham, Shearer and Cole up front (figure 69).

If, as I suspect, Glenn continues to play with five at the back then I think teams will try and work the ball wide against England. That's what Italy did until Maldini went off and they had some success. I would have two strikers up against England's back three at all times and I would get my width from somwhere else. If you leave your two strikers in on three defenders and you eventually get into a good position wide, behind the wing-back, then one of them is going to have to come across to the ball, leaving you in a very strong two-against-two position (figure 70). I would ask my wide midfielders and my full backs to work the flanks. I would ask them to really put those wing backs under pressure. You have to do that because this system leaves you no space down the centre. And, of course, if Beckham was in the side at right wing-back I would try and get my side attacking him, examining his defensive capabilities.

However, I think there will be a lot of managers trying to work out some way of beating this England side who won't be that confident. The strength of the current England set-up shows how English football is becoming more and more sophisticated. From the era of the middle to late 1980s, when we saw Wimbledon win the FA Cup, our game has developed. Whereas a lot of teams used to just put the ball into the danger area and see what they could get, teams are now

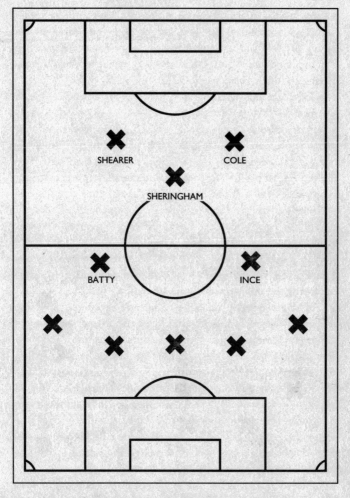

Figure 69: A more attacking England team within Hoddle's favoured 5-3-2 system

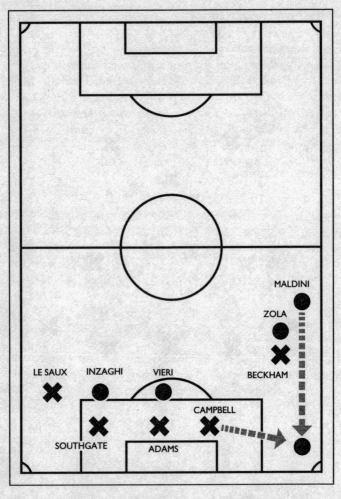

Figure 70: How England's five man defensive system can sometimes get stretched, and did against Italy before Maldini went off injured

more likely to neatly carve out their opportunities with precision and skill.

This England team can go very far in the World Cup. I think they can get to the semi-finals and then anything can happen. If they can stay away from Italy, France, Germany and Brazil until the latter stages then I don't see any problems for England. In fact, I predict that as long as they don't meet each other during the earlier rounds, England will be in the semi-finals alongside the teams I have just mentioned.

CHAPTER 17
Psychological Tactics

● ●

There are some tactics that simply can't be analysed with computer graphics or slow motion videos – psychological tactics. Things that get slipped to the press in the days leading up to a game, things that go on in the dressing room or in the tunnel before the teams emerge and things that happen on the pitch in the heat of battle, away from the beady eye of the referee or the television cameras. Football is as much about battles of the mind as it is battles of the boot.

During a game of football there are individual battles taking place all over the pitch. Private tussles between key individuals affect the outcome of the game. Clearly, the best way to win such a battle is to master the football. By getting the better of your opponent you will damage his confidence and the confidence of those around him and give yourself the edge for the rest of the game. However, when the ball isn't around all sorts still go on. Players like Ian Wright talk the whole time, trying to wind their markers up, trying to make them lose concentration or lure them into making a foul on the edge of the box. Neil Ruddock, playing for Liverpool at Old Trafford a few years ago, constantly turned down Eric Cantona's collar. Eric would put it back up, it was his trademark of course, but every time there was a break in play Ruddock would turn it back down. You could see Eric fuming. He was wound up.

When I was playing I was never one to take the mickey. I was always so focused on trying to score. But I would try to unsettle my opponents early on and let them know they were in for a battle today. I had a special tactic for whenever I was playing against Peter Shilton.

Shilts always used to say he hated playing against me. Now Peter was a great goalkeeper and I really admired him, but I always felt he was a little bit short. He was maybe two or three inches short of Schmeichel and I always thought he was vulnerable on crosses. So whenever I played against Shilts I used to say to the rest of the lads that the first thing they should do, wherever they were on the pitch, was to lump a great big high ball into the box. So in the first couple of minutes someone would lump it towards Shilts and I would go in and clatter him.

Then I would pick him up and, with a great big smile on my face, I would say: 'That's the first of many this afternoon, Shilts.' And he knew I was serious. Right from the first minute I was getting my mark in on him so that when the next cross came over he would be thinking about me as he went up for it. And maybe, just maybe, if he took his eye off it for a fraction, I would have a chance. And I remember beating him to a cross a few times. He always had one eye on me when the ball was coming into the box. I suppose this all sounds a bit brutal but in those days the game was much more physical, and it was an accepted part of the game.

But of course, it worked the other way too, and your marker would always try to get an early challenge in. They always gave you a physical battering and quite often they came right out and smacked you. In those days there weren't television cameras at every game, there was no video evidence, and all sorts of things went undetected. I remember my first local derby against Birmingham City when I was playing for Villa. I was only twenty years old and I was being marked by Joe Gallagher, a seasoned central defender who took no prisoners. A few minutes into the game the ball was down at the other end of the pitch, having gone out for a goal kick. I was walking back and as I looked at him he hit me. He threw a right hook which landed right on my chin and knocked me to the ground.

I got up and asked him what he was doing. He just looked at me and laughed. I couldn't catch my breath. I was absolutely astounded. I didn't know what to do. I was amazed that somebody could just turn round and punch you in the middle of a game with 50,000 people there and two linesmen.

In those days you really had to look after yourself and I soon learned a few tricks of the trade myself. I was talking about this to George Best and he told me a story about Denis Law from the days in the late 1960s when they were both playing for Manchester United. He said that although Law wasn't exactly a big man he could certainly look after himself. There was one game at Old Trafford when a centre back came hammering in from behind on Denis in the first minute, taking him out completely. About five minutes later United were defending and suddenly the ball got cleared to the halfway line and there was the centre back lying flat out near the centre circle. Denis, who was now twenty yards away looking as innocent as pie, had let him have it.

Things like that couldn't happen today because it would be caught by the television cameras or one of the hordes of photographers at the ground but people do still wind each other up. I remember Lee Dixon and David Ginola having a right old ding dong during a Coca-Cola Cup match between Arsenal and Newcastle a couple of seasons ago. The Frenchman finally snapped, lashed out, and got himself sent off.

Off the pitch, psychology is naturally a huge part of – some would say the major part of – management. A manager might be a tactical genius when it comes to devising formations or tinkering with his system, but if he's not getting the best out of his players then he's effectively starting every match with ten men. Managers basically have two main psychological aims, to get the best out of their team and to psyche out their opponents.

To get the best out of their team some will resort to hurling the half-time teacups around the dressing room to try and get better performances out of their players. My very first manager, Jim McLean, was a serial crockery thrower. When I was at Dundee United in the early 1970s he would actually go as far as humiliating players in the dressing room at half-time, in front of their team-mates, if they weren't doing the business on the pitch. He would rant and rave like a madman. There was never any china in the dressing room at Dundee United, it was always plastic because everyone knew what Jim was like. And you can bet your life there's no china in Manchester United's dressing room either because Alex is known as a thrower. In fact, I think he's calmed down a lot in recent years but he must be a ferocious man to play for if you are under-achieving.

Although Jim McLean was an unbelievable thrower of pots and cups, my next manager Ron Saunders at Aston Villa was not. Ron was quiet and very choosy with his words at half-time. He was more likely to talk to players individually rather than stand up and belittle people in front of the whole team. John Barnwell at Wolves was a bit of both whereas Howard Kendall at Everton was never a thrower of crockery, he was more one who thought that a few choice words would be enough.

When I was assistant manager to Ron Atkinson at Aston Villa we used to use the old 'good cop/bad cop' routine for the after-match team talk. If Ron went in with the big guns blazing, if he wanted to rant and rave at the players for one reason or another, then I would then go in afterwards all calm and relaxed to smooth it over. He would scream and shout at them and then I would go in and try to reinforce the message by delivering it to them in a different way. And if he went in light, I went in heavy. That was our psychology.

When we played Swindon away in the FA Cup in 1992 we were winning 2–0 and cruising until Tony Daley gave the ball away and Swindon scored. They hadn't even been in the game and we had gifted them a goal that got them right back in it. We ended up hanging on to win but as the players walked off the pitch Ron said to me: 'I'm going to go in and say "well done, lads," congratulate them and pat them on the back, but I want you to have a real go at Tony Daley.'

So he went in and congratulated the players. Then I went in and screamed at Tony. And suddenly all the boys were looking at me. They weren't joking around any more. We had given them all something to think about, something which we hoped they would learn from.

Good managers realise that all players are different. On the field every week there are eleven different personalities and while some might respond to a kick up the backside, for others the way to get the best out of them is to put an arm round their shoulder and have a gentle word.

I must admit a kick up the backside usually did the trick for me. I always responded to it. Managers could get the best out of me by giving me a challenge. I've always been one to rise to a challenge rather than disappear under it. Managers would say things like, 'This defender you're up against today is good, you'll not do too well against him.' And that would be enough to get me really fired up. I remember Ron Saunders would have a little word in my ear at half-time if he didn't think I had been performing. He would say something like, 'Have you been out drinking this week or something?' And he knew that would get me going.

But others who I've seen being given a public dressing down have completely folded. I've witnessed it in the dressing room. They just couldn't hack it and went into hiding. It made the situation worse. A manager has to know which players respond to a quiet word in their ear, an arm around their shoulder, a bit of goading, who responds to a public bashing and who responds to a private bashing.

Ruud Gullit's system of rotating his players when he was managing Chelsea, not telling even his own squad who was in the team until an hour or so before the kick-off, had two psychological aims. First of all he wanted to keep all his players on their toes to make sure that when they got their chance they played at their peak to try to retain their place. Secondly, his squad rotation made it virtually impossible for the opposition to lay plans to stop them. There was no point in a manager devising a masterplan to stop Zola only to discover when the teams were announced that he was on the bench. The only problem with having this kind of a selection system is that you are likely to get players unhappy at being left out if they have scored a hat-trick or kept a clean sheet the previous week, and I think that's very much what happened at Chelsea.

Jock Stein was the master of man management. As manager of Celtic during the 1960s and 1970s he won everything, nine league titles in a row, the European Cup, Scottish Cups, Scottish League Cups, and much of that success was down to his ability to wring every ounce of ability out of each and every one of his players. He knew them all inside out. He knew, for example, that his star player Jimmy Johnstone was terrified of flying so before a European Cup tie against

Red Star Belgrade at Parkhead in 1968 he told Jimmy that he wouldn't have to fly out to Yugoslavia for the return leg if he did the business that evening. So, what happened? Johnstone played out of his skin and inspired Celtic to a 5–1 win.

Stein found out what made his players tick, and consequently they would run through brick walls for him. He went to great lengths to get to know his players. I heard a story about one of the Celtic players from someone who used to drink in the same pub in Glasgow back in the 1970s. Apparently Stein would come round to the pub when the player wasn't there, find out who he had been talking to, what he had been talking about and how much he had drunk. This attention to detail made him a great motivator and a master of psychology.

I remember coming on as a substitute against Sweden in a World Cup qualifying match at Hampden when Jock Stein was manager. We were leading 1–0 at the time, it was a tight game and crucial that we won it. Anyway I got the ball, did a little jink into the box and a guy came over to tackle me. The ref blew for a penalty. We scored, it was 2–0 and that was that. After the game I was pleased as punch and when I was interviewed I was asked if the penalty decision was a bit harsh? 'Well, it might have been,' I said. 'I suppose if it had been given against us I'd have been really upset but, you know, we got it so I'm not complaining.'

When the next squad was named three weeks later I wasn't in it. I couldn't work out why. I had come on and done well. Then when the next squad was announced I was back in. When we got together Jock came up to me and said, 'You wondered why you weren't in the last squad, didn't you? Well don't go on television telling the world it was a harsh decision when it was a decision for us. Don't do it.' It was his way of showing me that he wanted winners in his team, that he only wanted players focused and fiercely determined to achieve success for Scotland.

Ron Atkinson is a very different kind of manager. He is a master of relaxing his players before a big game. With his non-stop one-liners he always gave the impression that he is unperturbed. Even if we were away at Old Trafford or Anfield it was like Scunthorpe to him. At least that was the impression he gave to the players. Deep down of course he knew it wasn't going to be easy at all but outwardly he was always confident. He hoped that the players would think that if he wasn't worried then there was no need for them to fret.

He also affected this calm, confident manner in front of other managers. I've seen him out in the corridor at Villa Park in front of all the opposition players, joking about and just showing them how relaxed and confident he was about the game. With someone who's a little nervous, like Roy Evans at Liverpool, he would say, 'Come here, Roy. What do you want, a brandy? Come on, it's only a football match. Have a brandy, sit down and watch the television for half an hour. Let the coaches get on with the players.' He's genuinely a great host of course, but there's also a certain amount of psychology going on there. He's putting on a show for the entire Liverpool team, hoping it will affect their confidence on the pitch, but don't ever let Ron's quips and jokes fool you. They hide a fierce and highly serious passion for the game.

Of course, there are other psychological games that managers play in public – for example, using the press and television to try to score points over an opponent and unsettle them before a big game. Alex Ferguson is the master of this, although if you ever asked him about it he would deny the thought had ever crossed his mind.

The incident that springs to mind is obviously the one during the run-in at the end of the 1995/96 season when Kevin Keegan blew his top live on television after Newcastle had played Leeds. Keegan was responding to Fergie's comments in an interview in which, if you read between the lines, the United boss seemed to suggest that he was concerned that Leeds and Nottingham Forest players might take it easy in their crucial matches coming up against Keegan's Newcastle. At the time Newcastle were just behind United in the title race with a handful of games to go after Fergie's team had overhauled a twelve-point lead.

After beating Leeds, Keegan just lost the plot. I was interviewing him after the game and I have never been so shocked by a manager's reaction. Normally Keegan was calm and relaxed after games, but this time he was like a man possessed and my shock soon went to sympathy and I wanted to end the interview. I knew it was making great television but I really felt for him and I thought that he was going to burst into tears, such was the emotion in him. He didn't seem to have any control over what he was saying, he had gone completely.

What had incensed him so much was Fergie's criticism of Leeds players for their lack of commitment over the season, saying if they could play with the passion that they had just shown against his United side (a game Leeds had narrowly lost 1–0 despite being down to ten men) then they wouldn't be struggling in the relegation zone. He said he hoped they showed the same effort and hunger in their next game...against Newcastle. Now I believe Fergie when he says that he was speaking up in defence of his good friend and then Leeds manager Howard Wilkinson, but he must have known how his comment would be interpreted. He also made a comment that he would be keeping an eye on Nottingham Forest's performance when they played Newcastle a few days after the Leeds game since they had agreed to be Forest's opponents for Stuart Pearce's testimonial match at the end of the season.

Personally I think Fergie was wrong to say what he did, and certainly it made everyone look closely at Leeds' performance in that next game. He denies he was playing psychological games but I'm pretty sure he knew what he was doing. From Kevin's point of view I thought it showed the passion of the man and an awareness of the other teams and the people around him. I didn't think there was anything wrong with that. If it hadn't been straight after a game then I think Kevin would have said what he said but with composure. It wasn't what he was saying that shocked everyone but the state he was in when he said it.

I think the Newcastle players would have been shocked, but in the cold light of day I think they would have had nothing but admiration for their manager. He was defending some of their own, the Leeds players and Stuart Pearce. I certainly don't think that this outburst cost Newcastle the title, but it showed everyone the pressure Keegan was under as an individual. That could have affected the players if he was losing it all the time, but the fact is I'm sure he went to training the following day and was his normal cheerful, confident self.

Alex Ferguson uses psychology more than any other manager. I think he has purposely created this 'everyone is against United' atmosphere. It's a kind of siege mentality that he has created and he uses it to bring everyone at the club closer together. He comes across as paranoid but, in fact, he's using psychology. I think he uses it every match when he sits on the touchline with his stopwatch. You're not telling me he's timing the match. He's saying to the referee: 'I'm watching you, and if you get it wrong I'm in your office.' That's psychology.

Managers often use the press to try and psyche out their opponents before a game. I remember Joe Kinnear getting a bit upset in 1997 when, before Wimbledon met Manchester United in an FA Cup game, there were all these stories in the papers about how Fergie admired Wimbledon. Kinnear thought Fergie was trying to get his players believing their own press. He much prefers it when the Dons are written off, branded a bunch of no-hopers and cloggers. The last thing he wanted was Fergie saying what tough opposition they would be. On that occasion, though, Fergie's psychological tactics didn't pay off as Wimbledon knocked United out after a replay. But he did the same when they were drawn to play Chelsea in the FA Cup in January 1998, saying what a great side they were, and then his team went and thrashed them 5–3.

But if a manager or a player does an interview slagging off the team they are playing or boasting of victory it can backfire on them. I've seen headlines and I've thought that if I was a manager I would pin the article up in the dressing room to get the players going. And if that doesn't work, nothing will.

One of the most bizarre psychological incidents I ever heard about was the work of Wimbledon owner Sam Hammam. Before an away game against West Ham in 1993 he sneaked into the Dons' dressing room with a box of magic markers and wrote all this anti-Wimbledon graffiti on the walls to make it look like West Ham had done it. The Upton Park staff who walked in and found the graffiti scrawled everywhere weren't too happy but Wimbledon won 2–0 that day.

The Dons, of course, are masters of that kind of psychology. Their famous ghetto blaster, taken with them wherever they go ensures that everyone knows when they're around and that they have absolutely no respect for anyone. When they played Liverpool at Anfield for the first time in 1987 each member of the team spat on the famous 'This is Anfield' sign at the entrance to the tunnel onto the pitch. By the time the last man ran out it was dripping with phlegm, and they won that day too.

CHAPTER 18
Manchester United 1997/98

● ●

MANCHESTER UNITED 3 JUVENTUS 2
1 October 1997 (UEFA Champions' League)
Old Trafford. Attendance: 53,428.

Manchester United: (4–4–2)

Schmeichel

G. Neville   Berg   Pallister   Irwin

Beckham   Johnsen   Butt   Giggs

Sheringham   Solskjaer

Juventus: Peruzzi, Birindelli, Ferrara, Montenero, Dimas, Pecchai, Deschamps, Tacchinardi, Zidane, Inzaghi, Del Piero

Before the game United manager Alex Ferguson had appealed for plenty of noise from the club's supporters, but Old Trafford was silenced by Alessandro Del Piero's goal for the Italian champions in the first minute. After the shock had died down, however, the Reds began to start creating chances of their own and after several near misses Sheringham finally brought the teams level seven minutes before half-time, charging in at the far post to head in Ryan Giggs' deep cross. From then on it was all United with the crowd roaring them on. Substitute Paul Scholes made it 2–1 in the sixty-ninth minute with a super-cool finish and then with a minute to go Ryan Giggs tore down the left wing at blistering speed and cracked a bullet-like shot past Peruzzi in the Juve goal. Zidane's neatly taken free kick in the ninetieth minute was a mere consolation.

CHELSEA 3 MANCHESTER UNITED 5
4 January 1998 (FA Cup, Third Round)
Stamford Bridge. Attendance 34,792

Manchester United: (4–4–2)

Schmeichel

G. Neville	Johnsen	Pallister	Irwin
Beckham	Butt	Scholes	Giggs
	Sheringham	Cole	

Chelsea: De Goey, Leboeuf, Clarke, Petrescu, Le Saux, Duberry, Di Matteo, Nicholls, Flo, Zola, Hughes

As tough a draw as they could have got, United had to get past the cup holders to progress in the FA Cup. In the end they didn't just get past them, they absolutely pole-axed Ruud Gullit's team. Looking sharper and hungrier in every position on the pitch, United were always in control. Beckham started the rout in the twenty-second minute, scoring from close range, then again five minutes later with a long-range free kick. Andy Cole blistered past Michael Duberry to fire in the third before half-time, getting another in the sixty-fifth minute before Teddy Sheringham made it 5–0 with a header on seventy-three minutes. Chelsea came back into the game but it was all over by the time substitute Vialli had scored their third.

Sometimes when I'm commentating on a Manchester United match I have to stop myself from taking off my headphones, sitting back and just admiring everything they do. The combination of skill, power, pace and passion that this team possesses is breathtaking at times. And the beauty of the team Alex Ferguson has created is in the simplicity of the system. As far as I am concerned, they are fast on their way to becoming one of the great sides in Europe.

The demolition of Juventus, European champions two years previously, beaten finalists the year before – showed exactly how far the team had come since the Italians had beaten them home and away in the Champions' League twelve months earlier. Perhaps helped by the fact that they went a goal down after a minute, United rolled up their sleeves and went for the jugular in a way I haven't seen an English side attempt in Europe since Liverpool were winning the European Cup virtually every season in the late 1970s and early 1980s.

With a squad brimming over with players of quite exceptional talent and temperament – many of them local lads and United supporters who have come through the club's youth set-up – Alex Ferguson's biggest tactical headache must be deciding who he leaves out of the team.

Fergie is a back four man. These days United always play with a back four but sometimes change tactics further up the field. Normally Alex plays a 4–4–2 system with a fairly tight midfield. In other words, the wide men (usually Giggs on the left and Beckham on the right) tuck in close to the central midfielders instead of spreading to the edge of the pitch. He will play with two strikers but with one of them (Sheringham or Scholes), playing slightly deeper than Cole or Solskjaer, linking with the midfield just as Eric Cantona used to (figure 71).

That's the basic United system, but Fergie does have a number of standard variations. If he's playing a team he feels he's got to be positive against he might only play three in midfield and go in with Sheringham, Solskjaer and Cole up front (figure 72). He does that a lot in home games in the Premiership. Alternatively, if he's got a really tough away game he might play 4–4–2 but drop one of his regular midfielders and bring in Ronny Johnsen to play a man-marking role.

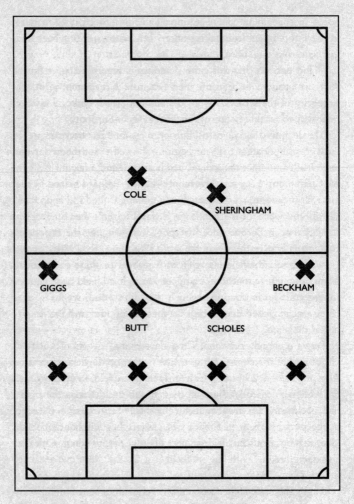

Figure 71: Manchester United's classic 4-4-2 shape

This is what he did in the Juventus game and to great effect in the Premiership at Anfield in December 1997, when Steve McManaman was shackled as United won 3–1.

They have so many options and so many good players that Ferguson can juggle his three main systems and the personnel to play within them before every game. Sometimes he will tinker with them even more because he knows he has players with footballing brains who will carry out his instructions to the letter. For tricky away ties in Europe, for instance, he might go for 4–4–2 but for the first twenty minutes or so Sheringham will drop into midfield leaving Cole up front on his own, so that they are playing with a 4–5–1 system to keep it tight at the start of the game.

After United beat Chelsea in the FA Cup in January 1998 I analysed their performance for *Monday Night Football* and I just couldn't get over the work rate of the team in red. It was phenomenal. The four midfield players were everywhere, but in a disciplined way. If you were to ask me to name a perfect midfield quartet, right at this moment in time, anywhere in world football, I would take the four that played in that game – Giggs, Scholes, Butt and Beckham.

I like United when Butt sits in and plays the holding role with the other three zipping into attack like a surge of electricity. They attack in waves of menace at high speed, but then they defend in the same way. Next time you watch United watch Ryan Giggs when he hasn't got the ball. He doesn't just use that pace he's got to roast full backs, he uses it to chase back, to harry and hustle like a demon when the opposition has the ball. They're all like that. Ferguson has made them into this ferocious midfield which works together when they haven't got the ball.

In 1995 Eric Cantona told me that he believed United had to change their style if they were to be successful in Europe. The game that Cantona used to explain his reasoning was the game United played in Gothenburg in 1994 when they took a 3–1 drubbing at the hands of the Swedish champions. What happened was that because the midfield was stretched all the way across the width of the pitch, they were exposed time and time again by creative midfielders who had time to look up and thread passes through. United played just as

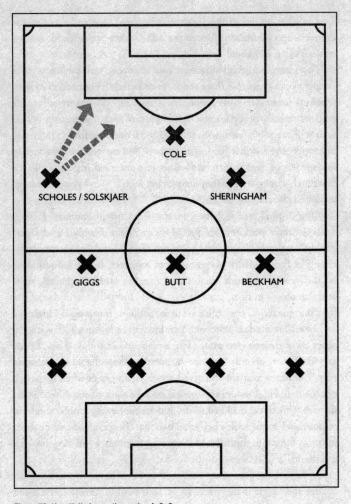

Figure 72: How United sometimes play 4–3–3

they would have done in the Premiership, with Giggs and Kanchelskis out wide and Keane and Ince in the middle with the defence pushing up looking for offside. But the quality of the opposition was such, that given time on the ball they found it easy to unlock the defence with through balls to runners from midfield. As I mentioned earlier, Cantona wanted Ferguson to play a pressing game similar to AC Milan's. I think that Alex has done that now, to an extent.

The current United side haven't gone all the way down this route, but they have learned to pressure the ball a lot better – not just in Europe but in the Premiership too. They've made themselves a much harder team to play against. They were always good going forward but the combination of Beckham and the new, mature Giggs is a totally different prospect to the old one of Giggs and Kanchelskis. They go wide when they have the ball and need to find space, but when they are defending they come inside to get it back. The entire United midfield works like this. They play free-flowing, scintillating football when they have the ball but they are all back fighting for it when they lose it.

Paul Scholes is one of the most gifted English players I have ever seen. He has the deftest of touches, incredible vision and the ability to finish as coolly as the most experienced striker in the world. But as if that wasn't enough, he tackles like Bryan Robson. With such deft feet, with such a sweet touch, he could be forgiven for leaving the crunching tackles to the likes of Roy Keane and Nicky Butt, but he doesn't. When the ball is bouncing around central midfield he's in there where it hurts, not just diving in for effect but wholeheartedly putting everything into the challenge, driven on by the urge to win the ball back and begin another relentless surge towards the opposition goal.

It's as though there are eight players in the Manchester United midfield. Fergie has four great defensive players and four great attacking players, all rolled into this awesome quartet. While David Batty at Newcastle is great in defensive situations but not so hot in attack, United have Nicky Butt who is equally adept at the holding role but doesn't go to pieces when he has a chance of scoring. The Manchester United four does absolutely everything you would want a midfield to do in a 4–4–2 formation. They have no peers in the Premiership at the moment.

They also have individual ability. But they combine it with this incredible willingness to work. The reason I like to see four in midfield is that the two wide men give protection to the two full backs. One of the easiest jobs in the world at the moment is being a full back at Manchester United. You very rarely get a full back in a one-against-one situation against United because invariably Beckham on the right or Giggs on the left have tracked back to protect Neville or Irwin. So you have this double protection right across the back four which is incredibly hard to break down. It's the platform for United's success.

Then when they have got the ball they have got just about every attacking option there is in football. On the right, Beckham can pick out passes and cross the ball as well as anyone. He might not be able to jink past players and beat them, but Giggs on the other side can do that. Giggs is a potent threat whenever he has the ball. Then centrally you've got Butt who I think will be a star of the England side for many years to come and even for the World Cup in France. Paul Ince and David Batty have got to watch out. He gets it, gives it, tackles like a demon, but has creativity and vision as well. And then there's also Paul Scholes who has a natural eye for finding space for the likes of Sheringham and Cole, and when these two have pulled the defence apart he's got a natural ability to find a gap for himself and get in there. They just have a wonderful balance in midfield.

The success of this team is one hundred per cent down to the brilliant management of Alex Ferguson and the coaching of Brian Kidd. All these players have ability, but the way that they translate that ability into the way they play has been coached into them. I don't think that Giggs, Beckham, Scholes and Butt would be the players that they are now if they were at any club other than Manchester United. These young players have had Fergie and his staff drumming it in week in, week out.

The midfield is the key to their play. When Manchester United played Chelsea in the 1998 FA Cup I could see, after twenty minutes, that if Ruud Gullit didn't change something then Chelsea would be in trouble. Ruud was playing 4–4–2 but he had no real protection in midfield with Mark Hughes and Roberto Di Matteo playing in the centre. They were getting overrun by Giggs, Scholes, Butt and Beckham. It was almost embarrassing. They desperately needed to go to five at the back because they were getting so badly exposed and put somebody into midfield who could compete with the likes of Butt and Scholes. I would have taken off Flo right away and brought on a defender. Then I would have put Hughes up front with Zola and taken Steve Clarke out of defence and stuck him in the midfield to give it a bit of bite. In fact Ruud made exactly that change at half-time but it was too late, they were already 3–0 down and the match was lost.

In the match against Juventus they transferred the way they play in England onto the European stage. The previous season they had played Fenerbahce of Turkey at such a slow pace that they never exerted any pressure. They tried to play a continental game, keeping the ball and stroking it about, and it just didn't work. They had a few chances but nothing much and in the eighty-fifth minute the Turks scored a lucky goal and United had lost 1–0. But when they played Porto in the quarter-finals they played at the kind of tempo you would expect to see them play at in the FA Cup. They absolutely destroyed the Portuguese champions, finishing 4–0 winners. Porto couldn't cope with it, and they were a side who had a hundred per cent record in their group games.

The tactics Fergie used against Juventus were very much the same as usual, 4–4–2, but he brought in Ronny Johnsen to man mark the Juventus playmaker Zinedine Zidane. But he didn't want Johnsen so close to Zidane that he never touched the ball. He just wanted him to keep an eye on him and pick him up whenever he came into the United half.

But goals often govern tactics. United conceded a goal in the first minute and so immediately any thoughts of being cautious or nega-tive went out of the window. They were on the front foot right away. In fact, I think losing that goal helped them in this game.

Another thing that inadvertently helped United was losing Nicky Butt late in the second half. With Butt and Johnsen in the midfield they were perhaps a little too defensive, especially after going behind, but as soon as Paul Scholes came on they looked a far more potent attacking force. Scholes was magnificent, scoring United's crucial second goal, and I'm sure Alex is desperately glad he was forced into making that change.

Often games like this hinge on the simplest of things. One of the roles of management is trying to identify a weakness in your opponents' game. We all looked at the Juventus team and said that they might be vulnerable in the air. It's very easy identifying something like this but you still have to exploit it. United did so brilliantly. It wasn't so much that they were just hurling balls into the box, they were manoeuvring themselves into areas from which they could play balls that would hurt the Italians. And that's exactly what they did to get the equalising goal just before half-time. Giggs played in a beautiful cross and Sheringham came in at the back post, got above two defenders and nodded a beauty into the far corner.

United have quality players. They are a group of lads who firmly believe that every time they go out they are going to win the game. When teams start losing games it doesn't take long for players to start poo-pooing the manager. But if the team is getting results because of the manager's tactics, then the players believe in themselves and they believe in their manager. This has been going on for so long now at United that they have a unity of confidence, and it's worth an extra player to them every time they run out onto the pitch. You don't get any self doubts when you are winning games. Players want the ball all the time.

A great side is one which is tough to play against, not one which is good to watch. Manchester United are the toughest. Despite some problems during the latter half of the 1996/97 season I expect them to have success in Europe before too long. Their commitment, their desire and the pressure they continually put their opponents under matches the unbelievable ability they have when they've got the ball. I honestly believe that they will go on to be mentioned in the same breath as the Busby Babes and the 1968 team, the first English side to win the European Cup. And with most of the players of English descent, Alex Ferguson must be right at the top of Glenn Hoddle's Christmas card list every year.

CHAPTER 19
The Way Four-Wards

● ●

Since writing this book I must say I have become less convinced that playing with a flat back four is the only way to achieve success in football. And it would be naive of me to say that no team that plays five at the back will ever win anything. But, having said that, I still think that when it's working properly and when you've got good players playing it, four at the back is the superior system. It's noticeable that most of the good teams in world football now play it. Be it France winning the World Cup or Arsenal winning the double in 1998, in the main, football's silverware-winning teams tend to have a back four as their foundation.

Arsenal's defence is the classic example of how effective a back four can be, and them winning the Premiership and the FA Cup double a week before this book was first published was vindication of what I was trying to say. The line-up of Adams, Bould (or Keown), Dixon and Winterburn have been playing together for so long they're as well drilled a defensive unit as you'll find anywhere in top-class world football. Arsenal's success in 1997/98 was built on these four players. The number of games they won 1–0 in that amazing final run-in – a run-in in which they went unbeaten for eighteen games – is staggering. It is also no coincidence.

Much of the credit for the success of this Arsenal defence must, of course, go to former Gunners' boss George Graham. Having called this book *Flat Back Four*, I had an interesting chat with George recently during which he said, 'Actually it wasn't a flat back four, it was really a curved back four'. By that he meant that in his Arsenal

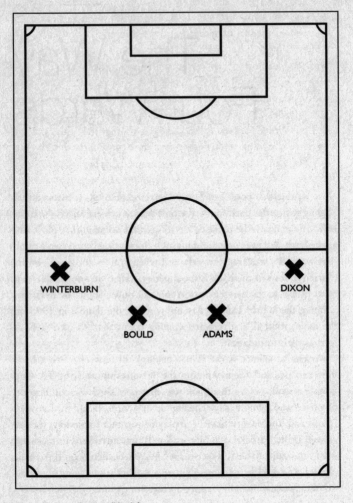

Figure 73: Arsenal's 'curved' back four.

defence the centre backs were flat, but both his full backs would always be a yard or two ahead of them (figure 73).

Basically what he was saying was that you can only play a back four offside trap properly if your centre backs are always the deepest of your players on the pitch. As soon as your full back goes deeper than your centre back then you're in trouble because then you cannot play offside. The centre backs need to know that they're always slightly further back than the full backs so that they can effectively work as a two-player offside trap. They can concentrate on each other's positioning and step up together without having to look over to the flanks to check that both full backs are also stepping up. Adams and Bould had to know that they could step up two yards without even having to worry that Nigel Winterburn and Lee Dixon were level with them (figure 74). And usually they did.

Arsène Wenger's current defence – which in terms of personnel is the same as Graham's – play slightly differently to this. But that's because of changes in the offside rules rather than any great tactical differences in the two managers' thinking. The change occurred when they amended the offside rule a few years ago. Basically what they said was that if you're running back towards your own goal you cannot be offside – you are deemed not to be seeking an advantage. Well it was these players that Arsenal always used to catch offside. When I was still playing the game the amount of time I used to spend running back towards my own goal getting flagged offside against teams like Arsenal was ridiculous.

When the law changed, Arsenal's defence realised that they couldn't step up as far as they had been because even if they caught the forwards offside if they were running back there would be no flag and they could be caught out by opponents running through from midfield. So what they had to do was stop running up the pitch as soon as they won the ball. They subtly changed it. They said, 'OK, we won't run out blind, but we'll hold the line'. What they do now is, if they're defending deep and the ball is headed out, the entire defence will push very quickly out to the edge of the eighteen-yard box. In the old days they would have kept going, to maybe thirty yards from their goal, but now they stop and defend from there. Then

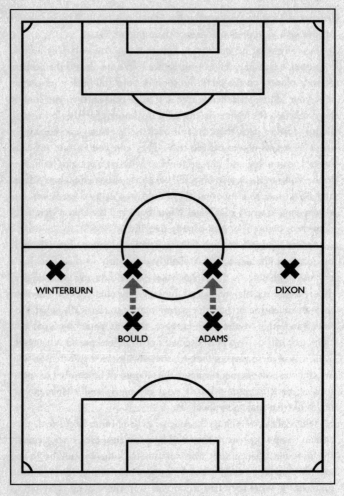

Figure 74: Arsenal's centre backs can step up without worrying that the full backs will play opposition players on-side.

if it is cleared another twenty yards forward, up to the halfway line, they'll come up another ten yards. They do it in stages now, not as one mad charge up to the halfway line.

But that rule change had already taken place by the time Arsène Wenger arrived at Arsenal. In terms of the basic defensive tactics I don't think he changed a thing. A lot of people don't realise that Wenger has always been a back four man. In fact it's funny to look at all the foreign coaches who have come into our game and play with four at the back. We thought all these continental managers would come here and play with sweeper systems and back fives, but here we are with Arsène Wenger playing a back four at Arsenal, Ruud Gullit playing a back four at Newcastle and Gianluca Vialli playing a back four at Chelsea to name just three.

And that's not all. I was working for Sky Sports at a Liverpool game not long after Gerard Houllier joined the staff at Anfield. Liverpool had just beaten Blackburn 2–0 and they'd been playing a back five. Gerard stopped me in the corridor after the game and said, 'Andy, I know you don't like this system and neither do I. I like to play four at the back but the players I have at my disposal are dictating to me how I must play. I don't have the staff'. In other words he admitted he was only playing a back five because he didn't feel he had the players good enough to play a four. His problem was that he didn't have a commanding centre back. It was great for me to have someone like him coming up to me and saying 'you're absolutely right, I like that system as well', and here was one of Europe's most respected coaches singing the praises of good old four at the back.

So much of a successful defence is down to the players being used to playing with each other. This was Arsenal's huge strength. That back four has been working on playing a back four on the Arsenal training pitch for close to ten years. It's repetitive and some say it's boring, but it works. Nigel Winterburn was in the press recently slagging off George Graham, saying that under him training was boring, it was dull. But I tell you what, had that back four not been drilled and drilled and drilled, then Nigel Winterburn might not have a closet full of medals.

As I have said, however, I don't think Wenger really had to do anything tactically with the defence. In terms of tactics, the interesting thing that happened at Arsenal during that glorious 1997/98 season was what happened in front of the back four.

At the beginning of the season Arsène Wenger lined up his side in a traditional 4–4–2 system (or if you look at it more closely a 4–4–1–1 with Bergkamp playing slightly deeper than Ian Wright, and later Nicholas Anelka). Ahead of the back four he had Parlour on the right side of midfield, Petit and Vieira in the middle and Overmars on the left. They were a straight midfield four. Wenger wanted Overmars to play as a traditional British wide midfield player, getting forward but also tracking back and dropping behind the ball when Arsenal lost possession (figure 75). But it wasn't working. I don't think Overmars was comfortable in that role. Coming from Ajax I think it was alien to him. He is an awesome offensive player but not really a defensive one.

But as the season went on the system changed. Now I don't know if it evolved naturally or whether Arsène Wenger made a point of changing the tactics, but with the same personnel the team evolved from playing this classic 4–4–2 to more of a 4–3–3 formation. Basically Overmars was relieved of most of his defensive duties and became much more of an attacking force. To compensate for this when Arsenal lost possession Patrick Vieira, Emmanuel Petit and Ray Parlour would tuck right back in and work as a barrier in front of the back four. These three worked across the field, doing the defensive midfield duties and acting as a platform for the attack when they won the ball. Overmars would come back and help out on the right every now and again, but his priority was to attack (figure 76).

I think this is what turned the season for Arsenal. Overmars began to have a serious effect in the top third of the pitch. By the end of the season he was scoring and creating goals for fun. Remember the one he scored away at Old Trafford? What a big, big goal that was. Then there was the opener in the FA Cup Final against Newcastle. It was a case of Overmars being let loose on the Premiership's defences while most of the time the other three midfielders held back and did a patrolling job to keep things tight in front of the back four.

Suddenly what happened was that instead of Bergkamp just having

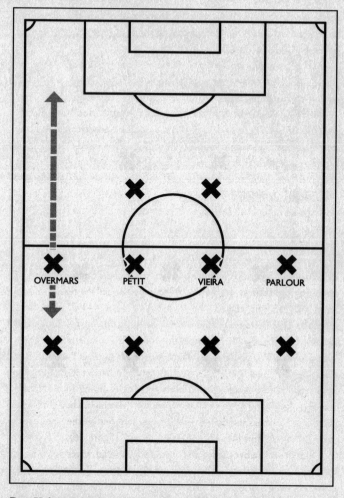

Figure 75: Arsenal's formation at the start of the 1997/98 season, 4-4-2 with Overmars playing a traditional right side of midfield role.

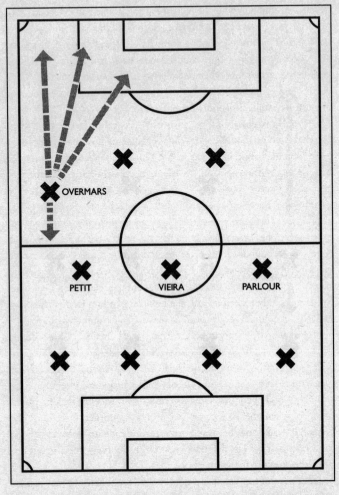

Figure 76: Arsenal's formation at the end of the 1997/98 season, with Overmars in a more attacking role in a 4-3-3 formation.

Anelka around him when he picked the ball up, he had Overmars too. And similarly when Petit or Vieira got the ball they had an Overmars option, not just the choice of a short ball to Bergkamp or a long one to Anelka. And since opposing defences now had a third attacking option to worry about when playing Arsenal, they were getting pulled further out of position and that, in turn, was creating more space for the creative skills of Dennis Bergkamp.

If you look closely at the games at the end of last season when Arsenal went on that unbeaten run, it's amazing how many goals they scored on the break. Defences would get sucked in and then suddenly Overmars or Anelka would be breaking straight back past them at incredible pace.

The way they played and the pace at which they played it meant that Arsenal would often end up with one against one or two against two when they were attacking. If Arsenal were defending, then Overmars would just hang around about thirty yards outside his own penalty area on the left hand side. Bergkamp would inevitably drift to the right and Anelka would sit in the centre circle. And if Overmars wasn't properly picked up and the ball came to him from a clearance he could very quickly turn, run at players and commit them.

I remember him scoring a great goal early in the double-winning season against Forest when exactly that happened. Forest had the game at 1–1, they were playing well and had Arsenal under a bit of pressure from a corner. And as they pushed forward looking for the winner nobody had picked up Overmars who was just lurking on the left. So when the ball came out from the corner Overmars was allowed to turn and, because Forest were so high up the pitch, he just pushed it past the last defender right on the halfway line and left him for dead to score the winner.

Like a lot of top European sides these days, when you play against Arsenal you almost have to be more disciplined in your defending when you're attacking. It sounds daft, but when teams have players with pace like Overmars, perception like Bergkamp and pace and finishing ability like Anelka then unless you mark them tightly and have a spare man as well when you're going forward they're going to rip you to shreds on the break.

This is the way the game is going generally now I think. Pace is more and more important, and hitting a team on the break is often the only way to score in a tight, technical game. One of the criticisms levelled against Liverpool in the past year has been that their build-up is too slow. They play too many passes. A bit like Newcastle became, I think, with David Batty in the side. If you look at the teams which have won the title in the last three or four years, they've all had a good pace to their attack. They've transferred it from back to front as quickly as they could.

I've often said that Manchester United are at their most dangerous when they're defending. With people like Kanchelskis, Giggs and Cole in the line-up during the last few years, they've always had great pace to build attacks on the break. The strange thing that happened at United in the 1998/99 season was that although they began the season scoring for fun as usual, they were soon conceding goals for fun as well. They scored three times in both matches against Barcelona in the Champions' League, but both times they let three in at the other end too. We started seeing them win 2–1 and 3–2 at Old Trafford instead of 1–0 or 2–0.

I think it was partly a question of personnel – Jaap Stam had come in and had to adjust to the English game – but I think there were tactical reasons for it as well. In midfield, whereas Arsenal have this great protection provided by Petit, Vieira and Parlour, when United play a midfield four of, for instance, Giggs, Keane, Scholes and Beckham, they're so geared up to go forward that at times they get stretched when they're coming back the other way. Usually it didn't matter because they would score more at the other end anyway. But that's how United's system differs from Arsenal's, even though they both play a back four.

The World Cup in France, too, was all about teams playing with a back four. Of the four semi-finalists at France '98 only Croatia played with a back five. Finalists France and Brazil and unlucky semi-final losers Holland all played with four at the back. France won the World Cup because of their defensive unit and their midfield, and because Zinedine Zidane had a good tournament. I always thought France could only win if their number 10 played well because they simply didn't have a front man good enough to score enough goals. When they didn't take Anelka I thought that even more. And without a potent attacking force they were always going to have to rely on not conceding many goals...so they played a back four.

France had two great centre backs in the form of Marcel Desailly and Laurent Blanc (with Frank Leboeuf taking over for the Final) and they dictated the play. They were decisive, confident and commanding. It was a classic back four: two towering centre backs and two full backs – Lizarazu and Thuram – who could defend but who were also excellent going forward. It worked perfectly, and ahead of the back four they had great protection from Emmanuel Petit of Arsenal and Didier Deschamps of Juventus which allowed Zidane to go and play his cameo role.

The French back four pushed up in much the way that Arsenal do, although they were clever enough to adapt to each situation. In the Final against Brazil, for instance, they were very conscious not to push up too far because they were worried about Ronaldo's pace. They didn't want him getting behind them. So they dropped off a bit to make sure that they never had to chase him, ensuring that at least he had to beat them. In normal games, however, they worked up the pitch as a really tight, really well-drilled back four and it worked sensationally well. They only conceded two goals in normal play all tournament against some decent teams and they were the only side to stop Brazil from scoring in a match.

So that was France's back four defensively. Solid, tight and well-disciplined. The beauty of it, however, was that whenever they won the ball every single member of that back four could use it to good effect. That's an added bonus for a coach who expects his defence, first and foremost, to defend. Often in the modern game you see centre backs who think they are players rather than defenders. It should be the other way round. The French side had great defenders like Desailly and Blanc who could also play the ball, not great players who can also defend a bit. That's dangerous. An awful lot of centre backs are guilty of thinking they are good players and forget the art of defending altogether.

And France needed this extra dimension because they didn't really have an attack. In the second round against Paraguay it was Laurent Blanc who charged forward to score France's golden goal and put them into the quarter-final. A key part of the team's tactics was Marcel Desailly stepping out of defence and bringing the ball with him. And when he did then Petit or Deschamps would just step into the back four to cover him. It was very well organised and it was crucial to the team's success.

In the season when they won the double we saw this kind of play coming from Arsenal's back four. Remember the goal Tony Adams scored against Everton on the last day of the season when he charged the full length of the pitch, latched onto a chipped through-ball by Steve Bould of all people and lashed it into the net? If you've got a defence that primarily defends but players within that defence who have the potential to join the play and influence things at the other end of the pitch then as a coach you are in dreamland – just as long as the team is organised enough to cover for any defender that charges forward.

With Leboeuf and Blanc, who played all but one of France's World Cup games, I think they had the perfect marriage of defensive and offensive skills. You couldn't fault them for the way they defended but they could also do damage to the opposition with the ball at their feet. When good defenders come away with the ball it opens up so much space for others. Teams will think they've got everyone marked, but when a defender comes marauding into the opponents' box it disrupts everything.

As the modern game of football gets more and more technical and defences and midfields become more and more organised, players coming from deep are becoming more and more crucial in opening up defenses. That's why I think Rio Ferdinand has a huge role to play for England in the near future. I hope it's as part of a back four, but I doubt it ever would have been under Glenn Hoddle. But even if it is in a five, I think Rio has an incredible role to play in England's future with his ability to step forward. Just look at some of the runs Sol Campbell made during the World Cup in France.

I think England have enough quality players to play any system they want. But I just think that playing with a back five when Glenn

Hoddle was manager meant that they could and did get exposed in areas where they wouldn't have if they'd been playing a four. As I have said earlier in the book, against good teams they were liable to get caught very bare wide because they only had the two wing-backs – one on the right and one on the left – on the flanks. Look at good teams playing against Glenn Hoddle's England and you'd always see them building up the play out wide. That's where England were vulnerable. Very vulnerable. They'd try and put the wing back under so much pressure that one of the centre backs had to come out and help out, leaving space in the box to exploit.

I didn't agree with Glenn when he said that you play too many straight lines when you play a back four. I think you play too many straight lines when you play a back five, because the only width you have is your wing backs who go up and down the pitch in one long straight line. They can't play anywhere else. Your three centre backs are the same, you never see them swapping sides. Just think about the options Glenn would have had if he had played a four (as Howard Wilkinson did as soon as he was handed the caretaker manager's role), there is quality all over the place. There's right backs like Gary and Phil Neville, at left back there's Graeme Le Saux, Andy Hinchcliffe or Phil Neville, at centre back there's the likes of Tony Adams, Gareth Southgate, Sol Campbell, Rio Ferdinand and Martin Keown. In midfield you've got the same. There's Anderton who can play wide right or central, Beckham who can play wide right or central, central midfielders like Butt, Ince and Batty. The left side of midfield is probably the only area where they might struggle – and maybe this is why Glenn played a five – but you've still got the likes of Steve McManaman or young Lee Hendrie as options and Darren Anderton can play there too.

And if the manager is still worried about the left side, England could even play a 4–3–3 formation with, say, Ince, Beckham and Butt or Anderton and then play three strikers with Shearer and Owen pushed up and Scholes playing just behind them. Glenn had these options but I don't think he would ever have used them. I'm sure part of that is the fact that everyone criticised him after the World Cup and he went into his shell a bit. I think the last thing Glenn Hoddle will ever do is admit he's wrong. After England drew 0–0 in Rome I think he showed an aloofness, a stubborn streak if you like, which suggested that even if it was as plain as the nose on his face he wouldn't change it.

Glenn did it his way and I had no objection to that. If you're a manager you have to manage in the way that you believe is right, and not the way others tell you to. I respect him for sticking to his values, I'm just saying that if I had been in charge I'd have done it slightly differently. It's a personal thing with me. Glenn believes in a five just as strongly as I believe in a four and that's fair enough. But I think four would be the players' choice as well. Most of them are playing a back four week-in, week-out and it must be very difficult for them to change to a five for one match every couple of months.

When Glenn was sacked, Howard Wilkinson came in and straight away reverted the team to playing a back four – playing three of the Arsenal back four (Adams, Keown and Dixon) in his first game against France. Howard clearly agrees with me. I'm not saying that playing a back five would have meant that England had no chance of winning anything. As I said before sooner or later a team will win a major tournament – be it Aston Villa winning the Premiership or England winning Euro 2000 – with a back five. All I will say is that when you look at the best teams in the world right now, they all play with a back four: France and Brazil, Real Madrid and Juventus, Manchester United and Arsenal. Name me a top side and I'm sure that they'll play with a back four. Maybe this is a coincidence but I don't think so. Maybe all the top coaches in world football have been reading this book!

Conclusion

• •

We've had the 'WM' formation, we've had *catenaccio* defending and the midfield diamond, so what's next? In a hundred years or so someone like me will probably be sitting down to write a book which dismisses the primitive notion of playing four at the back.

Maybe that person will have to call their book *Flat Back Two*, because if I can see anything happening in the future it is formations becoming narrower. Players are getting fitter and quicker and so they are able to cover more ground. In the future, then, perhaps two or three defenders could cover the ground currently covered by four. That might mean that we get a formation like 2–2–2–2–1–1. Then again I could be wrong and one day teams will be playing 4–4–2 on Mars.

Football in Britain – particularly in the English Premiership – has changed dramatically in the last few years. Most teams in the top flight of the English game are committed to playing a sophisticated, passing game rather than just hoofing the ball up to a big centre forward. Teams have realised that route one football can only get you so far, and that can only be good for our long-term hopes at European and international level where a certain amount of craft and subtlety is required to break down the very best defences.

The influx of foreign players and coaches has played a major role in this positive evolution of our football, although there is a danger that we are beginning to import quantity rather than quality. No one can doubt the benefits that English players at Arsenal have had from playing alongside the likes of Dennis Bergkamp and Patrick Vieira and under the forward-thinking regime of Arsène Wenger. But if it gets to the stage that First Division teams are fielding eight Norwegians simply because they are cheaper than equally talented

English players – something that is not inconceivable in the current post-Bosman ruling climate – then we will have a serious problem.

Let's hope that our young talent continues to emerge through the ranks and that my literary successor can add a few more sides from these shores to the list of great teams. For the one thing you will notice about the great teams that are featured in this book is that they were all full of great players. Hungary had Puskas, Hidegkuti and Kocsis, England had Moore, Charlton and Ball, Brazil had Pele, Carlos Alberto and Gerson and AC Milan had Baresi, Gullit and Van Basten.

Studying systems and tactics is all very well and – as the modern game gets faster and more organised – increasingly relevant, but at the end of the day it's players that win football matches, not lines on a blackboard or counters on the manager's desk. Put a side together with Pele, Maradona, Beckenbauer, Moore and Dalglish in it and they could play a 1–3–6 formation and man mark each other and they would still win every time. As the great Real Madrid player Francisco Gento once said of the Real side which won the first five European Cups between 1956 and 1960: 'We never had a blackboard, and hardly ever talked about our opponents. In the days of Di Stefano we just came to the stadium, put on our shirts and played.'

When I was playing for Rangers, before a game Graeme Souness wouldn't really give us any instructions. He would just say: 'What's the use of giving you tactics? I've bought you, you're the best players in the land. You're playing against players who aren't as good as you. All I'm asking is for you to go and play.'

Index